New Frontiers for Strong Forcing Openings

How to Split Your Strong Forcing Openings
2♦ for Hands with Spades
2♣ for All Other Hands

Text © 2010 Kenneth J. Rexford

Honors Books is an imprint of Master Point
Press.

Master Point Press
331 Douglas Ave.
Toronto, Ontario, Canada
M5M 1H2
(416) 781-0351
Email: info@masterpointpress.com
Websites: www.masterpointpress.com
            www.bridgeblogging.com
            www.masteringbridge.com
            www.ebooksbridge.com

**Library and Archives Canada Cataloguing in
Publication** has been applied for.

ISBN 978-1-55494-752-2

TABLE OF CONTENTS

FOREWORD..5

INTRODUCTION...9

THE TWO DIAMONDS OPENING 13

WHEN RESPONDER HAS FOUR OR MORE SPADES 16
When Responder has a Weak Hand without Shape
....*18*
When Responder has a Weak Hand with Shape ...*25*
When Responder has Any Other Game-Forcing
Spade Raise..*27*
Possibilities for the Immediate Spade Raise in the
Real World..*31*
WHEN RESPONDER HAS FEWER THAN FOUR SPADES.48
The Artificial Two Hearts Waiting Response........*52*
    Spades as the Longest Suit...............................52
    Minor-Spade Canapé Bids 53
    Handling the Specific 4-4-4-1 and 4-4-5-0 hands
   57
    Some Hands Featuring a Canapé Minor Rebid.59
    Heart-Spade Canapé Hands: 63
    Freak Two-Suiters..69
    One Possible Optional Treatment 71
    Balanced Hands 72
The Positive Responses...*73*
    Extra Discussion of the 2♠ Heart Positive 75

THE TWO CLUBS OPENING 83

WHEN RESPONDER HAS A BUST HAND 85
The 2♠ Rebid for Hearts..*85*
Other Options after a Bust 2♥ Response..............*88*
    Opener Bids Two Spades to Show Five
    or More Hearts 88
    Opener Bids Either Minor Naturally.88

THE POSITIVE RESPONSES WITH A SUIT OR SUITS 89
The Positive Major Flags............................ 89
The Positive Minor(s) Relay........................ 90
THE WAITING POSITIVE 91
Kokish Two Hearts by Opener 94
 Responder's Alternatives to Kokish 2♠ 95
 When Opener has the Super-Strong Balanced
 Hand 96
 When Opener Has the Unbalanced Hand with
 Hearts 97
 Some Practical Analysis.......................... 97
The Minor-Heart Canapé Two Spades Rebid...... 98
 If Responder has a Heart Fit................... 99
 If Responder Has No Fit for Hearts 107
  With the 1-4-4-4 hands........................ 109
  With Four Hearts and a Longer Minor....... 109
  The Heart-Minor Canapé with a Spade
  Fragment 110
  The Heart-Minor Canapé without a Spade
  Fragment 111
Straight Minor Rebids.......................... 118
The Jump to Three Hearts...................... 125
The Jump to Three Spades 125
The Jump to 3NT............................... 128
A Note on 6-5 with the Majors.................. 129

**WHEN OPENER SHOWS A STRONG,
BALANCED HAND** 133

A QUICK NOTE AS TO RANGE 133
WHEN OPENER STARTS WITH TWO DIAMONDS AS HIS
OPENING 134
When Responder Has a Minor and Slam Interest
.... 136
When Responder has Interest in the Majors...... 140
 The 3♦ Jacoby Transfer....................... 140
 The Modified Puppet Stayman 3♣................. 141

WHEN OPENER STARTS WITH TWO CLUBS AS HIS
OPENING 143
  The Jacoby Transfer to Hearts, and Texas
  Transfers *145*
  The Modified Puppet Stayman 3♣ after the Initial
  2♣ Opening..*146*
DEALS FROM ACTUAL PLAY 148
WHEN OPENER HAS THE SUPER BALANCED HAND AND
BIDS 2NT AFTER KOKISH 159
  Three Spades as a Minor-Oriented Asking Bid ..*160*
  Modified Puppet Stayman..........................*160*
  A few from actual play *161*

HANDLING INTERFERENCE............................**165**

INTERFERENCE AFTER A TWO DIAMOND OPENING ..165
  Responder's Options After 2♦ if Doubled..........*166*
  Responder's Options After a 2♥ Overcall..........*167*
  Responder's Options After a 2♠ Overcall..........*168*
  Responder's Options After a 2NT Overcall........*168*
  Responder's Options After Higher Interference.*168*
    Special Idea after 3♣ or 3♦ Interference –
    Submarine Style 169
    After 3♥ or Higher................................170
  Opener's Options *170*
INTERFERENCE AFTER A TWO CLUBS OPENING 171

FOREWORD

Back in 2006, I published my first bridge book, *Cuebidding at Bridge: A Modern Approach*, a book that I had written for myself as a method of putting my thoughts down on paper. I had no real intention of actually publishing it, until my wife suggested that I send it in to Master Point Press to take a look. I was quite tickled and surprised at their interest, and ultimately at the enthusiasm that many had for my ideas.

One major question was raised by Sandy Long in his review of my book in *W A Bridge Focus* (an Australian bridge newsletter), namely whether I could come up with some solution for the ultimate problem, as I had not done so yet. The ultimate problem was 2♣. I, of course, knew this, as does everyone else. The Achilles' heel of natural systems is that extremely preemptive strong 2♣ opening, which has yet to be resolved with any response and rebid structure that actually works. When Opener has 21+ HCP, the partnership should be happy, not dreading the ridiculously daunting task of even agreeing on strain.

I mean, think about how difficult these auctions can be. With two-suiters, most do not even try launching into 2♣ sequences, sometimes opening with a non-forcing one-bid and praying for a response, even then unsure how to put these unexpected points on the table. Minor rebids after a 2♣ opening are so difficult that most require about a 4-loser hand at worst to even try that bid, and some avoid the call with more than three losers. We all know how difficult 4441 hands are, but how about 4-3 or 3-4 in the majors with a five-card minor that is not that impressive a suit? When I played Precision and a canapé system, these obvious problems gave rise to a joke of ours where we defined a 2♣

opening for the opponents as "Strong, artificial, and preemptive."

So, why did I skip that whole subject in my book? Simple. There is no good solution, in my opinion, within the confines of the 2♣ opening.

I decided, however, to re-think the issue. What about splitting a 2♣ opening into two bids? What about making 2♦ a second strong, forcing opening? This has been tried a few times, with sometimes strange methods attempted and discarded. Is there something better?

The initial response I would often hear while thinking this through is that you would then give up any other meaning for a 2♦ opening, like "weak." That seems to be a silly objection. Precision players, who like to taunt natural players for their silly 2♣ opening, also must forfeit this type of meaning for 2♦. Canapé players also have this result, except in the Neapolitan system, which is a messed up, inconsistent canapé approach anyway, just to save that silly weak 2♦ opening. Even people who use a natural approach often ditch a weak 2♦ opening for some other meaning, whether Flannery, the dubious "Mini Roman" convention, Mexican 2♦, or any number of other pet meanings for a 2♦ opening. So, the idea of using two distinct strong, forcing openings, 2♣ and 2♦, could not possibly fall to that sort of objection.

Next issue. Having decided to split the 2♣ opening into two separate openings, what should be the difference? Many over the years have tried various ideas, but most have failed because the distinction between these two openings was not one that answered the basic problem that exists with the 2♣ bid – strain selection difficulties. If the issue is strain, then it seems to me that the two bids should each handle some set of hand types that is wildly different from the other. I thought about complicated ideas, sometimes even branching into wild thought like parity differences (open 2♣ if I have three odd suits but 2♦ with three even suits). Obviously, I was in danger of losing my mind.

It then occurred to me, somewhat as a Eureka moment, that perhaps it would work well to have a 2♦ opening show spades, with a twist inspired to some degree by my prior and lengthy experience with canapé bidding. What if a 2♦ opening handled any hands with five or more spades or with four spades and a longer second suit? This seemed to solve some of the most glaring of 2♣ problems, as it eliminated out some of the problem hands immediately.

The basic structure would be fairly simple. Let's assume partner bids 2♥ as his response, the cheapest and most frequent response. If I have five or more spades, I could rebid 2♠ and be back to a normal sequence, except that I happened to open 2♦ instead of 2♣; but who cares what I opened? However, if I held a longer, second suit, I just bid that as my rebid, actually showing two suits in this process (the original four spades and this other longer suit). Easy, and easy is good.

But, then it occurred to me that the use of a 2♦ opening to handle these hands frees up the 2♠ rebid after a 2♣ opening as unnecessary to show spades and perhaps useful for some other meaning. That could then handle the parallel hands of four hearts and a longer minor, the second major problem pattern, as I could bid the minor after partner rebids a semi-forced 2NT.

In other words, 2♣ - P - 2♦ - P - 2♠ - P - 2NT - P - [3minor] was an easy sequence to show hearts with a longer minor. Now, I was getting somewhere.

After working through the bidding and realizing what was needed, a few things became apparent. This solution solved almost every conceivable strain issue, and only the most freakish hands required bids above

3NT to settle the strain issue. Furthermore, we could actually agree trumps early enough to actually cuebid effectively. Most importantly, though, the approach was logical, easy to remember, and easy to handle. I think that this is the solution to the ultimate problem posed by Sandy Long.

As I started to put all of this together, I eventually discovered that Mats Nilsland, of Sweden, had come up with a very similar idea[1] and played with this technique for a few years with Anders Wirgren, also of Sweden. His idea of a two-way opening structure also included almost this same 2♦ opening, although he had a much more complicated rebid and response structure that was an extremely artificial methodology to capture every conceivable pattern with extreme and frightening detail. I believe that my structure is vastly superior, not in the grabbing of every possible hand pattern, but in the practicality of a simple and easy to remember approach, because I use as much natural bidding and parallel structure as I can.

What follows is my idea.

You will find, as you read through the material, that I discuss both a basic structure and also some gadgets that I recommend for taking advantage of the structure in slam sequences. Obviously, your own preferences for slam bidding should govern how you explore slams. I truly believe that the basic structure is of benefit to intermediate players without all of the bells and whistles, but, being who I am, I cannot help but mention these as well.

Ken Rexford
October, 2009

---

[1] I never have achieved a complete translation of his Swedish-language system notes, but I was able to decipher the general meaning.

INTRODUCTION

One of the lingering problems with natural bidding systems like Standard American and 2/1 GF is that the strong 2♣ opening is a mess. Back when I played a lot of strong 1♣ systems, we used to joke that a standard 2♣ opening should be defined as "strong, forcing, artificial, and preemptive," because of the amount of space it deprived for the side "blessed" to have a very strong opening hand.

We all know the problems. Consider one typical scheme, where a strong 2♣ opening has a response structure where 2♦ shows a game-forcing hand and is "waiting" and where a 2♥ response shows an immediate double negative. The problems are similar with a simple waiting 2♦ response, and probably worse with control steps.

Several problem hands and situations are well-known. After the negative 2♥, Opener has a difficult time if he holds a strong hand with five hearts. If he bids 3♥, this is essentially forcing to game. Thus, a 2♣ opening with five hearts is essentially a game-forcing opening. That induces a lot of very heavy 1♥ openings, or an occasional fly-by-night game.

How about when the strong hand is a minor two-suiter? You open 2♣, hear a response, rebid 3♦, and then what? Because you have to bid at the four-level to show the second suit, you tend to open 1♦ with some extremely strong hands when you have a minor two-suiter.

What about minor rebids generally? How long must Responder's major rebid be? If four, how do we find the 5-3 fit? If five, how do we find the 4-4 fit? Again, the minor-based 2♣ opening is extremely strong, and accordingly the one-level minor opening could be extremely strong, as well.

We can do better. We can fix the problem.

In the pages that follow, you will be introduced to a new convention, a 2♦ opening that shows a strong, forcing hand with at least four spades. This will make a strong 2♣ opening usually deny four spades. That simple change to the system will accomplish a truly remarkable feat. Every primary problem with a strong and artificial 2♣ opening will be solved, as well as many unimaginable advances made to your bidding generally.[2]

Among the amazing results are the following:

1. You will have no problem handling strong hands with four hearts and five or more of a minor. In fact, you will be able to agree hearts at a level low enough for all calls above 2NT to be cuebids. You will also be able to agree the minor, instead, at a level below 3NT, and often with space for some cuebidding below 3NT.

2. You will be able to set spades as trumps when Opener has four and Responder has a fit, at a level low enough for all calls above 2NT to be available to help look for a slam, no matter what Opener's pattern may be. If the major is not agreed, you will be able to agree any longer second suit held by Opener below 3NT.

---

[2] This new convention is actually not all that new. Mats Nilsland introduced this concept as part of his Super Standard system. My version is very similar to his version.

THE TWO DIAMONDS OPENING

The first major change to the system is ditching the Two Diamonds opening that you currently use. Instead, Two Diamonds will be a second bid to show a strong, forcing, and artificial opening, roughly equivalent in strength to a standard Two Clubs opening. However, on some patterns where you would be loath to open Two Clubs because of rebid problems unless you were extremely strong, you will not be as troubled. Thus, in a sense, you might have a slightly lower "minimum" for some hands. In other words, that "grown up" view that you learned where 21 HCP is not always enough to open 2♣ will now change to a new view where some 20 HCP hands and 19 HCP hands will merit a strong, forcing opening, for the unexpected reason that using the strong, forcing opening will actually be easier than the one-level opening.

Two Diamonds shows roughly the same strength that a standard Two Clubs opening shows, except that it promises four or more spades. Why four or more spades? Well, one answer is that, "It just does. Don't worry about it." For the theoreticians, if you figure out why this works so well, let me know. I believe that my experience with canapé bidding may have suggested this solution, and I never understood why canapé bidding is so effective either, but it just is. There is probably some sort of mathematical "proof" to explain this, but understanding why this works so well is not all that important. Just sit back and watch what happens when you have one strong, forcing opening dedicated to hands with four or more spades and the other therefore tending to deny four or more spades. This opens up an amazing amount of inference and an impressive number of tools.

Because almost all hands with four spades go through a Two Diamond opening (the exception being

super-strong balanced hands), you will open Two
Diamonds any time you have five or more spades, but
you will also open Two Diamonds with perhaps
unexpected holdings, like any 4-4-4-1 hand with four
spades and some other stiff, as well as hands with four
spades and a longer second suit.

You will learn that Responder's first option is to
immediately agree spades. Responder will be able to
bid 2NT with promising hands, 3♥ with weak hands,
and even a splinter with minimal game-forcing hands
and support.

You will also learn that a 2♥ call by Responder
is waiting and denies four spades, allowing a bid of the
spade suit after this denial of four spades to be used as
an artificial bid if Opener does not show extra spade
length.

After Responder bids 2♥, Opener will be able to
describe balanced hands with a fairly normal 2NT, but
those auctions will be enhanced because of what we
already know about Opener's spade length, and about
Responder's spade length for that matter.

When Opener has a regular, five-card or longer
spade suit, he will rebid 2♠ after Responder's waiting
2♥ call, and these auctions will be fairly standard, like
your grandparents used to play. Similarly, Opener's
minor rebids and heart rebids will be normal and natural,
showing five-card suits, except that we will know that
the possibility of a spade fit is out because Responder
will have denied four spades. Plus, these calls are not
truly "normal." For example, a 3♣ rebid after a 2♦
opening will be a canapé auction. Opener will be
showing a long club suit, but he will have already shown
a four-card spade suit and will have denied a fifth spade
by not rebidding 2♠. This 3♣ call, therefore, will show
a club-spade two-suiter, but with longer clubs. The
same will be the case for a 3♦ or 3♥ rebid.

This all works together. When Opener starts with a 2♦ opening, he has four or more spades. With a balanced hand, he will rebid 2NT. With five or more spades, he will rebid a normal 2♠. With a spade canapé hand, meaning four spades and longer in a second suit, Opener will first check on the spade fit. If no spade fit is found, he will then bid his longer second suit.

All of this is explained further, in the following table.

The Opening Bid of Two Diamonds

Shape Requirements:

    If Balanced:

        22-23 HCP, with 4-5 spades

    If Unbalanced:

        5+ spades,

        4-4-4-1 with any singleton except spades,

        or

        Four spades, with a longer second suit

Strength Requirements if Unbalanced:

    Normally, 21+ HCP

    Frequently lighter with good playing strength

Life could be great after a Two Diamonds opening. Opener has already shown at least four spades. If Responder also has at least four spades, we have a fit, and that fit is in a major. Let us set trumps immediately and get to business!

There will be three ways to immediately raise spades.

First, Responder might have a weak hand, anywhere from a dead bust piece of trash to barely worth a game raise. With those hands, Responder will bid 3♥, a sort of "weak transfer" to Opener's spades.

Second, Responder might have this same trashy hand, which is not all that unexpected after a strong, forcing opening, but he might have the nice additional feature of a stiff or void on the outside. If he has that hand, Responder will immediately splinter into his shortness.

Third, Responder might actually have something. If he does, which would be nice, he makes a 2NT call, agreeing spades. You might think of this as somewhat like a Jacoby 2NT raise, showing four-card support and game-forcing values, obviously needing less to force game after this strong, forcing opening.

These three options are described in more detail next.

Short Summary of Responses With Support

Three Hearts is a Weak Raise – Not Forcing to Game

Responder may pass 3♠ by Opener

Responder may raise 3♠ to Game to show a Bare Minimum with no singletons or voids.

Weak Splinters – Spade Support, Shortness, but Weak to Moderate

4♣ shows a weak to moderate game raise with club shortness

4♦ or 4♥ shows a moderate game raise with shortness in the bid suit

3NT shows a weak game raise with shortness in diamonds or hearts

The *Two No Trump* "Jacoby" Raise

4+ spade support and GF values

Too strong or otherwise wrong for a weak to moderate splinter or 3NT

When Responder has a Weak Hand without Shape

Having a fit is nice, but perhaps Responder has a piece of junk. Four spades, but little else. With either a bust hand or a bare game force, Responder bids three Hearts, a transfer to spades. Remember, Opener has shown spades but he had not yet bid them. So, Three Hearts is the weak raise of spades, one below spades to ensure that Opener bids spades first. A weak transfer to the trump suit, if you will.

When Responder bids Three Hearts, he is showing spade support (four or more spades) and either a bust hand (with which he plans to pass if Opener bids only Three Spades) or a hand with just enough to raise to game but not much more, and no shape (no singleton or void). The weak hand could be as ugly as perhaps ♠ x x x x ♥ x x x ♦ x x x ♣ x x x.[3] The bare minimum raise to game hand should feature no more than two of the top three spades or one of the top three spades and a minor King (a side minor Ace would be too good). The reason that Opener must have a minor King as his only possible control, if he has any side control, is because of Opener's options, explained next. However, one point of clarification is that Responder could have one side Queen instead of a side Ace or King, but he should not have both and should not have two side Queens. This is a weak bid. With even the trump Queen, a side King, and another side Queen, Responder would be too good for a 3♥ call. Similarly,

---

[3] If you think that this is too weak, tell me how you were stopping short of 3♠ anyway, after a normal 2♣ opening. If you could stop short of 3♠, you would probably also not be in spades (by passing 2NT) and would have missed the fit.

two side Queens plus one of the top three spades is too much.

When Responder bids Three Hearts, Opener has a few options.

First, Opener might want to sign off opposite the bust hand. If so, he completes the transfer by bidding Three Spades, which is not forcing. If Responder has the bust hand, he will definitely pass. If Responder has the hand with minimal game-forcing values, he will instead raise to Four Spades and reveal nothing more about his hand.

Second, Opener might have a hand where game is a good bet even opposite the bust hand but where slam is not a good bet even opposite the minimal game-force hand. If so, Opener will jump to Four Spades after the Three Hearts transfer, a super-acceptance of himself, in a sense.

Third, Opener may have slam aspirations even opposite this bad news. If he needs more information, Opener can bid Three No Trump to ask what Responder has. If Responder has the bust hand, he re-transfers back to Four Spades by bidding Four Hearts. Opener is on his own from there. If, however, Responder has the bare minimum game force, he can either cuebid a minor King (4♣ or 4♦) or may bid 4NT[4] with no minor control

---

[4] If you want a little more science, Responder could bid five of his doubleton if he has five spades. Responder could bid 5♠ with only four spades and no doubletons. Responder would then bid 4NT with only four spades but a doubleton. If Responder bids 4NT, Opener can ask for the doubleton by bidding 5♣, with Responder responding 5♠ to show a doubleton club, the "missing" doubleton. Remember, though, that all of these calls deny a side minor King but promise two of the top three spades.

but with a generally decent hand otherwise (meaning, per our definition, two of the top three spade honors). In either event, he cannot have a heart control because there is no good and easy way to show the heart control and to keep Opener as Declarer. With that hand, he would raise spades in a different way, explained later.

The risk to this approach, of course, is that it forces Responder to bypass the four-level when he has no minor control. This leads us to the fourth option for Opener. If Opener needs a specific minor King for slam purposes, he can bid 4♣ asking for the club King or 4♦ asking for the diamond King. In either event, if Responder has that King, Responder will bid 4NT (or use the scheme suggested in the footnote); 4♥ would be a re-transfer denying that King. If Responder hears Four Clubs asking for the club King and lacks it but does possess the diamond King, he will bid Four Diamonds.

Consider a few examples:

Opener: ♠ A K Q J 2 ♥ K ♦ K 6 ♣ A K 10 5 4
Responder: ♠ 10 9 8 7 5 ♥ 10 7 2 ♦ Q 8 3 ♣ J 9

Opener will start 2♦, promising four or more spades. Responder will bid 3♥, a transfer showing a

---

After the signoff (4♠), Opener's 4NT could then have modified responses, rather like Backwards Roman Blackwood:

5♣	= One key card, with a red doubleton (Opener can bid the one he wants as an asking bid, if it matters)
5♦	= One key card, with a doubleton club
5♥	= No key cards, without the trump Queen
5♠	= No key cards, but with the trump Queen

weak or bare game force with four or more spades, establishing the fit. Opener needs very little for game, but slam is out of the question. If Opener decides to bid the game, he will bid 4♠ and keep Responder's hand undisclosed, as well as his own. If Opener is conservative and bids 3♠, Responder's fifth spade and side honors are probably enough to force the game. He will simply raise to 4♠.

Opener: ♠ A K Q J ♥ K 9 7 6 ♦ A 3 ♣ K Q 7
Responder: ♠ 10 6 5 4 3 ♥ 8 3 ♦ 10 8 2 ♣ J 8 2

Opener again opens 2♦ and hears 3♥ from Responder. Opener suggests a signoff at 3♠, which Responder passes.

Opener: ♠ A K Q J 10 ♥ Q 3 ♦ A K Q 6 2 ♣ A
Responder: ♠ 9 8 5 3 2 ♥ 8 5 2 ♦ 9 8 7 ♣ J 7

Again, 2♦ - P - 3♥ starts the sequence. Opener has a powerhouse and needs nothing except a heart control. However, Responder showed a balanced hand, and, if he has a control, it is in a minor. Opener resigns to 4♠. Switch Opener's red suits, and Opener could bid 4♦. Because Responder does not have the diamond King either, he would reject that slam try by re-transferring back to 4♠, bidding 4♥. Had Responder held that diamond control, he would bid 4NT, or answer immediate RKCB if that is the style.

As an example of how this works nicely, consider a problem deal from the 2007 United States Bridge Championship, where one of the favorites ended up in 3NT, a contract that has no hope, rather than 4♠, a contract that has a lot of play and that succeeded in practice at the other table:

```
                      ♠ A Q 10 7 3
                      ♥ K Q 8 2
                      ♦ A Q
                      ♣ A 4

        ♠ 8 2                        ♠ K 5
        ♥ A 10 9 4                   ♥ 7 6
        ♦ K J 9 3                    ♦ 10 7 4
        ♣ Q J 8                      ♣ K 9 7 5 3 2

                      ♠ J 9 6 4
                      ♥ J 5 3
                      ♦ 8 6 5 2
                      ♣ 10 6
```

North deals and opens 2♦, planning to rebid 2♠ if necessary. However, Responder has a bust hand with four spades. So, Responder bids 3♥, agreeing spades, but planning to pass if Opener cannot bid anything more than 3♠. Opener, playing teams, and realizing that there is a nine-card or longer spade fit, but no chance of slam, bids 4♠ and reaches the correct contract.

Another example, this time from the 2008 Yeh Brothers Cup:

```
                    ♠ A K 8 7 6
                    ♥ K Q 9 2
                    ♦ K 3
                    ♣ A Q

    ♠ 3                          ♠ J 9
    ♥ A 3                        ♥ 10 8 5 4
    ♦ Q 10 9 8                   ♦ A 7 6 2
    ♣ J 10 7 6 4 3               ♣ 9 5 2

                    ♠ Q 10 5 4 2
                    ♥ J 7 6
                    ♦ J 5 4
                    ♣ K 8
```

West deals and passes. North opens 2♦, planning to rebid 2♠ to show five or more spades, and then later show the hearts if necessary.

However, Responder has spade support with a single and lonely minor King on the outside. Accordingly, Responder bids 3♥ to agree spades and show a weak hand without a stiff, but intending to bid 4♠ if Opener signs off at 3♠. If Opener shows interest in the possible minor card by bidding 3NT, Responder will show the club King (4♣).

Opener has a hand that would normally justify a slam probe. However, he now knows that Responder has no Aces on the side and at best the club King. No slam is possible. But, a game surely seems to be a reasonable bet at IMP scoring. 4♠ is reached anyway, no matter who bids it ultimately.

A third example, from the 2008 Vanderbilt, shows how our methods can avoid goofy results from interference:

```
                    ♠ A Q 8 7 3
                    ♥ A K
                    ♦ J 9
                    ♣ A K 5 4

   ♠ K                        ♠ 5 2
   ♥ J 9 7 3                  ♥ Q 10 2
   ♦ K 10 8 7 6 2            ♦ A 5
   ♣ Q 6                     ♣ J 9 8 7 3 2

                    ♠ J 10 9 6 4
                    ♥ 8 6 5 4
                    ♦ Q 4 3
                    ♣ 10
```

After a pass from West, North opened 2♣ using standard methods. This looks like a simple deal, with North-South having a nice, easy auction to 4♠. East, however, was Justin Lall, a brilliant young pro player who has a liking, as do most young stars, for getting into all sorts of places they might not belong, including at the bridge table. So, he decided to toss his opponents a problem by intervening with a cute 3♣ overcall.

This worked its magic, as South doubled to show a bust hand (with any possible shape) and North, having no clue where this belonged, opted to pass with his unexpectedly strong club values. Justin somehow escaped with a two-trick set and won a few IMPs for his effort.

This development was cute, but we would have had no problem with this barrage. South, hearing our 2♦ opening instead, would know that North had at least four spades. After a 3♣ overcall, South's trashy hand but well-placed stiff in clubs will result in an easily bid spade game. Even an insane 5♣ overcall would not block South from seriously considering a 5♠ raise, which is safe on the layout.

When Responder has a Weak Hand with Shape

Responder might also have a weak hand, as far as HCP are concerned, but some shape. With something like ♠Q x x x ♥x ♦x x x x ♣ x x x x, Responder is willing to play in Four Spades opposite a strong, forcing opening showing four or more spades. He can show this type of weak, unbalanced hand by splintering immediately. These calls deny any honor-based side controls (no side Aces or Kings) and generally deny much at all on the side (maybe one Queen, if that).

With a bare minimum game force because of a stiff or void in a red suit, Responder bids Three No Trump over the Two Diamonds opening. The reason that this shows a red-suit splinter is again because of Opener's options and because of the need to keep Opener as Declarer. Opener, if interested in the shortness, can bid 4♣ to ask, with Responder simply bidding his short red suit (4♦ or 4♥). Note that this, again, keeps Opener as Declarer.

With a slightly better minimum and a red-suit stiff or void, Responder can jump to 4♦ or 4♥. This shows something more, perhaps two of the top three trump honors and a side stiff or void. However, one of the top two spade honors and five-card trump support, a void, or a side Queen might also justify the more aggressive immediate splinter.

Keep in mind that Responder should not have two of the top three spade honors and either a void or a side Queen, however, as that would be too good for the weak splinter. Responder also should not have both the Ace and King of trumps with five of them and a stiff, as that also would be too good.

The club-based splinters, weak and intermediate, both are handled by bidding 4♣. If Opener cares to ask, he can bid 4♦. With a minimum, you can re-transfer to 4♠ by bidding 4♥. With the higher splinter (again, only somewhat better), you can bid 4NT, or perhaps use some sort of immediate-answering structure[5].

A few deals for study:

Opener: ♠ A K Q J ♥ J 10 ♦ A K J 3 2 ♣ Q 10
Responder: ♠ 10 8 5 3 2 ♥ 3 ♦ 8 7 6 5 ♣ J 6 4

Opener starts with 2♦. Responder has spade support and a stiff heart, and accordingly he bids 3NT, showing a stiff or void in a red suit and a bare minimum. Opener hopes that it is a heart stiff, but there is no reason to ask. He just bids 4♠ and hopes that this makes.

---

[5] I would suggest, for the scientists, that Responder could immediately answer somewhat logically, as follows:

4NT   = Ace-Queen or King-Queen of trumps. 5♣ would ask which, in steps: 5♦ for K-Q, 5♥ for A-Q.

5♣   = Club void. Opener's 5♦ asks what trump honor, with 5♥ showing the Queen, above 5♠ showing the Ace or King and a feature.

5♦   = Side diamond Queen, Ace or King of trumps

5♥   = Side heart Queen, Ace or King of trumps

Opener: ♠ A K Q 3 2 ♥ 4 3 2 ♦ A K Q 8 ♣ A
Responder: ♠ 10 9 7 4 ♥ 7 ♦ 7 4 3 2 ♣ Q 10 6 3

Opener starts 2♦ and hears a 3NT call from Responder. A heart stiff might just be enough. 4♣ asks, and Responder shows the golden hand by bidding 4♥. If Opener has held ♠ A Q 4 3 2 instead, but Responder had held ♠ K 10 7 4, an immediate 4♥ by Responder, the strong splinter, would have done the trick.

Opener: ♠ A K Q 3 2 ♥ A ♦ A K Q 8 ♣ 4 3 2
Responder: ♠ 10 9 7 4 ♥ Q 10 6 3 ♦ 7 4 3 2 ♣ 7

Now, Opener again opens 2♦, but Responder's 4♣ call does not specify the overall strength of the hand. That is not a problem when Opener's spades are solid. Had Opener held ♠ A Q 4 3 2, instead, he could bid 4♦ after 4♣ to ask Responder about his general strength. With the actual hand, Responder would bid 4♥ as a re-transfer declining the slam invite; with the missing spade honor, Responder could bid 4NT, or answer immediately as described earlier.

When Responder has Any Other Game-Forcing Spade Raise

With any hand that is too strong or otherwise inappropriate for either a Three Hearts transfer response or an immediate or delayed (through 3NT) minimum splinter, Responder will agree trumps by bidding Two No Trump, setting spades as trumps and showing four or more spades, like a Jacoby 2NT raise, if it helps with memory. Once spades are agreed, the partnership can begin searching for cards for slam.

It is not critical what approach the partnership uses here. Some may want Opener to complete his pattern. Some may want to treat this 2NT call somewhat as if it were a Jacoby 2NT call. Some may want to start with their own cuebidding style. The key is that spades are agreed at an amazingly low level and that you are well ahead of the field.

For my part, I would suggest that the lack of any real definition by Opener suggests using an approach that is initially somewhat pattern-based. With a two suiter, whichever may be longer, I think that Opener should bid his second suit, bidding 3♠ to show a second suit that is clubs. After that call, everything else should be cuebidding. Tactics might justify Opener calling a 4441 or 4432 hand a "two suiter," depending upon what he wants to learn and what the predicted auction will be, and Opener might even describe a three-card fragment as a "second suit" if he thinks that this will somehow enhance the predicted cuebidding sequence.

The thinking as to Opener's decision on how to proceed should be along the lines of facilitating a cuebidding sequence with the expectation that Opener, the hand clearly with the greater values, should probably be captain of the auction. However, Opener's method should set parameters for what cuebids mean. For example, consider the auction where Opener has opened 2♦ and Responder has supported spades by bidding 2NT. If Opener also has a diamond suit and bids this next (3♦), the definition of Responder's cuebids will be tailored such that he will not cue shortness in diamonds but may cue any of the top three honors, including the Queen. Side suit cues, in clubs and hearts, will not be the Queen but may be shortness. Opener is equally interested in the diamond Queen whether his hand features the spade ♠ A K J x and diamond ♦ A K J x x or his spades are five cards in length and his diamonds only four in length. So, there seems little need to define which is longer. With some hands, though, Opener might for this reason define a 4-4 holding within a balanced hand as if a two-suiter to encourage low-honor cues in a specific side suit and to avert shortness cues in that suit, and Opener might even do the same thing with respect to a fragment suit, such as with a hand like ♠ A K J x ♥ A K x ♦ x ♣ A K Q x x, where a 3♥ call might enable finding the heart Queen and where the club suit is solid anyway.

I also think that this basic idea can be somewhat improved by having Opener bid 3♠ to show a club suit with two (or all three) of the top three spade honors and bid 3NT with a club suit but only one (or none) of the top three spade honors. This is because the 3♠ call robs the partnership of the ability to cuebid trumps unless Opener simultaneously shows his club suit and his spade control contribution.

I would have a 3♣ call be a waiting call, meaning possibly simply a convenience bid to start the cuebidding as low as possible, but also used for any hands with balanced shape or spades only.

I also think that jumps also offer opportunities for further description. A good technique would be for a jump by Opener to show a stiff but a minimum, perhaps with 4♠ showing the stiff heart.

I would use Serious 3NT, with Opener's 3NT call (he is always serious) tending to be tactical (to get under 4♣) but with Responder's 3NT tending to show really good internal honors, meaning trump honors or honors in Opener's shown suit, if there is one. I would use 4♥ as Last Train to Clarksville by Opener. A 4♥ call by Responder should be a transfer to 4♠ if somehow no one has actually bid spades yet, or a true cuebid otherwise. In theory, Responder could bid 4♠ as a Last Train bid if 4♥ would be a transfer.

However, as I will often mention throughout, some of the sexy stuff is not necessary and is simply offered as my thoughts for the wild people out there, ready to try anything and everything.

Whatever your approach, though, you may want to make it a purpose to have Opener bid spades first, to right-side the contract. For example, suppose you are using my approach, where a 3♣ call by Opener is waiting. Responder might cuebid 3♥ to show a heart card and to deny a diamond card. Opener's next call should probably be 3♠, waiting and showing nothing other than that it was time to grab the contract. Had Responder bid 3♦, instead, showing a diamond card, Opener might bid 3♠ to deny a heart card but grab captaincy. If Opener were to hold a heart control, he would not jump past 3♥ just to grab the contract; he would cuebid 3♥. Responder might then bypass 3♠ and continue cuebidding, not denying anything by his failure to cuebid or otherwise bid 3♠.

You might also decide that an unexpected grab of the spade contract by Responder shows something specific, like two Kings on the side. Whatever you do, have a general understanding with partner concerning this issue. Keep this concern in mind until the matter is resolved, which may require a Roman Key Card auction.

Or, I suppose some of you might just say, "The Heck with That!" and not worry about who declares the contract. In the end, that might not be such a bad idea. This preserves the ability to cue 3♠ as a trump cue, a worthwhile goal. In actual practice with a friend of mine, I ended up in that camp rather quickly.

Possibilities for the Immediate Spade Raise in the Real World

In the last round of the 2007 Bermuda Bowl Finals between USA I and Norway, USA I found a route to a making 6♠ when Norway languished in 4♠, 11 IMPs to USA I. The main difference seems to be that USA I valued up Opener's hand to a 2♣ opening, perhaps because of the three useful Tens and the high control count. I would also upgrade Opener's hand, but I would open with a strong, forcing 2♦ opening:

$$
\begin{array}{l}
\spadesuit\ K\ 9\ 8\ 3 \\
\heartsuit\ 3 \\
\diamondsuit\ 7\ 3 \\
\clubsuit\ K\ 9\ 8\ 5\ 4\ 3
\end{array}
$$

♠ 6 5		♠ Q J 7
♥ Q 9 6 5		♥ J 8 7 4
♦ K Q 8 6		♦ 10 9 5 4 2
♣ 7 6 2		♣ Q

$$
\begin{array}{l}
\spadesuit\ A\ 10\ 4\ 2 \\
\heartsuit\ A\ K\ 10\ 2 \\
\diamondsuit\ A\ J \\
\clubsuit\ A\ J\ 10
\end{array}
$$

In the successful USA I sequence, South opened 2♣ in first seat and then rebid 2NT after a 2♦ response from North. It appears that North then bid 3♣ as some sort of major ask, yielding a 4♣ call from Opener, presumably 4-4. North then transferred to set trumps (4♥ - P - 4♠) and single-handedly just decided to move toward slam, it seems. Maybe 4♣ showed something promising.

31

Our sequence would have been much better, with much more discussion before the ultimate decision. Opener would start with a 2♦ opening because he has four spades (and not a super-strong balanced hand). Responder, with four spades himself, would now immediately set spades as trumps. Because he has better than a bust and better than a simple minimum game force, and better than a splinter would show, he bids 2NT.

Opener, using my preference, would probably make a 3♣ rebid, waiting. This starts the cuebidding. Responder bypasses 3♦ to deny a diamond control and but bids 3♥ to show a heart control.

South, holding both of the Ace and King of hearts, will on this hand know that the control is a stiff or void. Because Responder did not splinter, Opener knows that Responder has something nice over there, presumably a club card. However, Opener cannot cuebid 3♠ because he does not have two of the top three spades. He also cannot justify cuebidding 3NT as Serious 3NT because he has a contextual minimum and does not want to make the decisions here. He has a hand that he upgraded (because of the high control count and 10's) just to be able to open 2♦, with A K 10 x opposite a known stiff and only the first round of trump control. So, Opener instead just makes a cooperative 4♣ cuebid. Because Responder already denied a diamond control, 4♣ by Opener also inferentially promises a diamond control.

So, to recap, here is the difference between our auction and the auction for USA I. North for USA I knew that his partner held a balanced hand and probably strength that looked like 22-23 HCP's, with a possible upgrade from 21 HCP's. North also knew that South held 4-4 in the majors, and perhaps a good hand contextually. Our North, however, would know that his

South held a strong hand with at least four-card spade support, not two of the top three spades, a diamond control, and a club control, with probable wasted values in hearts. What North does at this point is a function of judgment and the state of the match. USA I was down substantially and desperate, so they gambled and won that small skirmish. On a better day, that would be unnecessary. However, our auction gives Responder much more information with which to decide what to do.

An amazingly illustrative hand came up a bit earlier in Shanghai during the Semi-Finals of the 2007 World Championships. Twelve of the best players in the world sat East after a pass from North with this collection:

♠ A K Q 10 ♥ A J 2 ♦ -- ♣ A Q 7 6 5 2

What would you open, using standard methods?

Well, this hand is extremely troubling for most folks, including competitors in the Semi-Finals of the 2007 World Championships. Only 20 HCP's, but the shape is powerful, providing only three losers by Losing Trick Count. A 2♣ opening followed by a 3♣ rebid is problematic, however. Although the general strength is about right, it is a tad on the light side for such strong action. There is little ability to explain the unbalanced nature of the hand, which may cause problems exploring the majors. Will partner's new major calls promise five cards, making a spade fit difficult to locate, or showing four, making a heart fit difficult to locate? If partner raises clubs, our auction is very high. If partner bids a major, he will declare the suit, and we will have little room to explain our pattern, if any. A 1♣ opening might be better, but what if this is passed out? Partner needs very little here for great things.

The full deal:

```
              ♠ 7 6 5 4
              ♥ K 9 5
              ♦ 7 6 4 3
              ♣ 9 4

♠ J 8 3 2                      ♠ A K Q 10
♥ 10 7 3                       ♥ A J 2
♦ A K Q 10 2                   ♦ --
♣ 3                            ♣ A Q 7 6 5 2

              ♠ 9
              ♥ Q 8 6 4
              ♦ J 9 8 5
              ♣ K J 10 8
```

Norway tried the 2♣ opening and lost 15 IMP's. The auction had a predictable start. 2♣ by East, 2♦ waiting by West. 3♣ by East, 3♦ by West, possibly waiting as well. 3♠ by East. West now bid 4♥, presumably a general undefined cuebid, just showing support for spades and general slam interest without enough to go further, like a Last Train bid. East, knowing that West had "something" but not sure what, leaped to 6♠. West, knowing that East had "something," and thinking that he had "something plus a smidge," bid 7♠, failing. Quite impressive for our future champions.

South Africa had a typical auction for those opting to shoot low. East starts 1♣ and prays. West obliges and bids a normal 1♦. East sighs relief and jumps to 2♠. West shows extra strength and support with a 3♠ call[6]. West cues his two top clubs by bidding 4♣ (I would consider this hand strong enough for a Serious 3NT call, but maybe that tool was not available or would show something different for South Africa). West shows something more than expected in diamonds by bidding 4♦, and East, who cannot stand it any more, launches into trusty Roman Key Card Blackwood, 4NT. After the meaningless 5♣ response (apparently South Africa uses 1430 responses), East is still without knowledge of anything useful and bids 5NT as a punt bid. West likes his hand, but he is not sure why, and guesses 7♠. The same disaster.

Look how nicely this deal is handled by using the 2♦ opening. First, East has no misgivings about opening the hand 2♦. If Responder can support spades, life is good. If not, East has a simple 3♣ canapé rebid, a call that will show the location of at least nine of his cards, not just six. Plus, East knows (and you will also know this shortly) that Responder would then be able to support clubs below 3NT by bidding 3♠ or could show hearts (3♥) with confidence that a heart call by Responder shows five of them. If Responder were to make the expected 3♦ rebid, Opener would be tickled because he can complete his own entire pattern below 3NT by bidding 3♥. So, a 2♦ opening is far from something to be feared and avoided. All things will be grand (forgive the pun).

East opens 2♦, strong, forcing, artificial, and promising at least four spades. This works wonders, as Responder does have four spades and can agree spades immediately by bidding 2NT. That call by West also shows something better than minimum.

---

[6] Presumably West could have bid 2NT as an artificial relay to 3♣ before bidding 3♠ if he had a weak hand.

Opener now bids 3♠, showing that clubs is his second suit, whether a shorter suit or a longer suit; remember, we reserve 3♣ for "punt" cuebidding starts. Opener also, using my preferred methods, will have shown that his spades are good, as 3NT would show the same hand (clubs as second suit) with less impressive spades (one or none of the top three spades).

Responder will not bid 3NT (Serious 3NT) because he lacks anything of interest in either black suit, as far as honors are concerned. Instead, he will simply cuebid 4♦, showing the diamond control while bypassing 4♣ to thereby also deny a club honor.

At this point, there are a couple of ways for Opener to proceed. However, one thing is certain – Responder did not cuebid 4♣ and therefore does not have the club King. All roads with that information seem destined to stop at the small slam.

The point, however, is not so much in the specific auction and final contract that would have resulted. The point is that the 2♦ opening made this East hand, a nightmare for the Semi-Finalists, a rather easy hand to bid.

Another deal from Shanghai:

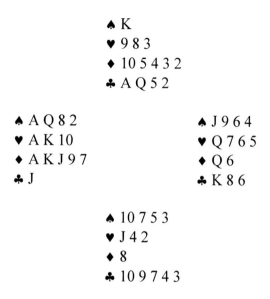

♠ K
♥ 9 8 3
♦ 10 5 4 3 2
♣ A Q 5 2

♠ A Q 8 2   ♠ J 9 6 4
♥ A K 10   ♥ Q 7 6 5
♦ A K J 9 7   ♦ Q 6
♣ J   ♣ K 8 6

♠ 10 7 5 3
♥ J 4 2
♦ 8
♣ 10 9 7 4 3

Sitting West, with 22 HCP's and great shape, you want to open a standard 2♣, but a little prediction of the difficulty of the likely auction and problems with exploring the majors induced a lot of West players to open 1♦. If partner does not pass 1♦, the first hurdle is crossed. However, it will be difficult to catch up in explaining to partner how truly strong this hand is.

In the Venice Cup, Denmark tried one solution to the problem and opened 2♣. After partner bids 2♦ (waiting, possibly game-forcing), the solution was for West to jump to 3♠ to show four spades and five or more diamonds. In practice, this worked somewhat, because the spade fit was found.

However, two problems were apparent. If East had held one fewer spade and one more heart, the heart fit would have been lost. Second, East has a nice collection of cards but no real way to distinguish a minimal spade preference from a decent spade acceptance.

We would have no problem with this deal. West starts with 2♦ and accomplishes the first goal immediately – showing the four-card spade suit. In practice, East's four-card spade holding makes this hand very nice, because he will bid 2NT to immediately agree spades and to allow a lot of space to further explore the chances of a slam. Opener can and will then bid 3♦ to complete his pattern before cuebidding starts (which allows Responder to later cue the diamond Queen if he gets the chance).

What if East had held the "death holding" of three spades and five hearts? For us, that could not be a problem. After East responds 2♥, waiting, West will canapé into diamonds, showing four spades and five or more diamonds, just like Denmark showed. However, because we have accomplished this goal *below* 3♥, Responder would then be able to bid 3♥ and we would find the heart fit.

What if East had held three spades, the same four hearts, and now a third diamond?

Again, we have no problem. East responds to 2♦ by bidding 2♥ and denying a spade fit. West bids 3♦ to show the hand with longer diamonds and four spades. Both East and West now know that we do not have a spade fit, and this fact allows us to use an artificial 3♠ call from East to agree diamonds below 3NT.

The end result, then, is that we no longer see this pattern as a problem. For West, he knows that we can agree spades with a 2NT call from East, agree diamonds below 3NT if East does not have a spade fit, and even find the heart fit with space to cuebid.

The 2♦ opening also can be powerful in competition. Consider yet another deal from Shanghai:

<pre>
                    ♠ J 9 4 3
                    ♥ A
                    ♦ Q 10 9 7 5 2
                    ♣ Q 2

    ♠ 10   ♠ 6 5
    ♥ Q 9 8 5 3 2   ♥ 10 7
    ♦ A 6   ♦ 8 4 3
    ♣ K J 9 8   ♣ 10 7 6 5 4 3

                    ♠ A K Q 8 7 2
                    ♥ K J 6 4
                    ♦ K J
                    ♣ A
</pre>

South, dealer, opened 2♣ at many tables, with West overcalling an interfering (and frisky) 2♥. This did not cause much of a stir in the end, because East could not further this interference after North passed. North-South were fortunate that the huge fit for East-West was in clubs.

Consider the difference that our 2♦ opening would have had on the auction. First, we would have found the spade fit one bid and almost a full level lower, even after the 2♥ overcall. Responder would have been able to bid 2NT over a 2♥ overcall to agree spades. In fact, as you can see, even a 4♥ overcall would not create much of a problem.

Second, assume for the sake of argument that Responder only had three spades and that Opener had six diamonds and four spades. After 2♦ - 2♥ - P - P, he would be able to bid 3♦, showing at least nine of his cards and already knowing that spades did not provide the source for a fit. That last fact would, incidentally, allow Responder to raise diamonds artificially with a 3♠ call, below 3NT, and even in competition.

Thus, the fact that 2♦ promises four or more spades immunizes us from a lot of preemptive actions by the next seat.

A nice deal from the 2004 Olympiads:

```
              ♠ 9
              ♥ J 7 6 5 2
              ♦ 7 6 5 4 2
              ♣ 10 4

♠ A K Q 5                    ♠ J 8 6 4 3 2
♥ Q                          ♥ A
♦ K Q 3                      ♦ 10
♣ K Q 9 6 2                  ♣ A J 8 7 5

              ♠ 10 7
              ♥ K 10 9 8 4 3
              ♦ A J 9 8
              ♣ 3
```

In practice, the Netherlands opened 1♣ to get a 1♠ response and a 2♥ overcall by South. West then launched immediately into 4NT, heard a 6♣ jump reply by East, whatever that meant, and bid 6♠.

Now, arguably one might still open this West hand 1♣ even if using our approach, as the stiff heart Queen does not seem to carry its full weight. The shape is nice, though. For the sake of discussion, let us assume that West opts the high road of a 2♦ opening.

East will immediately support spades with a 2NT call. Now, interference by South will be less troubling, because West will already have put his strength on the table and because the spade fit will already be located. East should have little trouble deciding what to do.

With standard methods, strong hands with some 4441 pattern are difficult. The 2♦ opening can often mitigate this problem. Consider these two hands, from the 2008 European Bridge Team Championship:

Opener: ♠ A K Q 2 ♥ A J 6 5 ♦ Q J 9 5 ♣ A
Responder: ♠ J 9 4 3 ♥ K Q 8 2 ♦ 4 ♣ 6 5 3 2

Opener would never dream of a 2♣ opening using normal methods. A 4-4-4-1 hand is known to be a real rebid nightmare. The result was a 1♣ opening, enticing a potential disaster when Opener's LHO held ♠ --- ♥ 9 4 ♦ A 10 8 6 3 2 ♣ K Q 10 9 4.

In practice, one South player overcalled this distributional monster with the less-than-brazen two notrump, giving East and West plenty of room to stumble-bunny around and eventually land in 4♥. The full auction was a mess, though. After the 2NT call, Responder apparently lacked tools for this sequence and this hand (as do I) and opted to pass (as would I). North picked clubs, which East doubled for takeout (good decision). Responder cuebid 4♣ as a wise choice-of-games call, doubled by North and redoubled by Opener, perhaps suggesting possible slam interest with a first-round club control. The auction ended at 4♥.

Imagine the problem if South's first intervention is a 4NT call. Opener would be pinched into a wild guess.

Our auction, in contrast, is easy. East opens 2♦ and immediately puts the four-card spade suit on the table. If South never intervenes, East and West will cuebid back and forth after the initial spade agreement by West (2NT), no one ever taking the plunge.

However, suppose South intervenes with a leap to 4NT, showing the minors. West bids an easy 5♠ and jokingly says later, "What was the problem for everyone else?"

West might then carry the joke further by commenting that he considered a 5♦ cuebid in support of spades a tad rich for this hand. Actually, that is the one risk here. West knows too much and might easily get aggressive and cuebid 5♦. Fortunately, however, East does not "have it" and will resign to 5♠ even after that carrot is dangled.

Of course, you have probably noticed that 5♠ may well go set because of bad luck. I always have bad luck. Why are the majors not stacked in hearts, instead???

It is always important to remember that good slam bidding is not defined as getting to slam when others do not. That's easy – just overbid slam hands. Good slam bidding also means avoiding slams when the slam cannot be made or is anti-percentage.

Another deal illustrates the benefit of quick spade agreement.

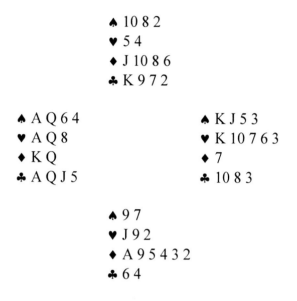

♠ 10 8 2
♥ 5 4
♦ J 10 8 6
♣ K 9 7 2

♠ A Q 6 4   ♠ K J 5 3
♥ A Q 8   ♥ K 10 7 6 3
♦ K Q   ♦ 7
♣ A Q J 5   ♣ 10 8 3

♠ 9 7
♥ J 9 2
♦ A 9 5 4 3 2
♣ 6 4

In the Semi-Finals of the 2009 Vanderbilt, four failing slam contracts were reached at all four tables. 6♠ was bid twice, 6♥ once, and 6NT once. Both a Strong Two Clubs opening and a Strong One Club opening were employed to handle this deal; neither "science" nor "natural" prevailed. But, with the club hook failing, all slams fail. Can we do better?

We can, if West opens 2♦, immediately announcing the spade suit. The hand is perhaps strong enough for a Kokish sequence, but the K-Q tight in diamonds could be downgraded, especially with no pip support beyond one 8 and especially considering how much better auctions are when we know something about spade length immediately.[7] That would be rewarded with a 2NT spade raise, showing extras (the

---

[7] OK. I admit it. I want to jam the 24 HCP hand into 22-23 to make a point.

hand is too good for a "moderate" splinter because the heart card is the King). Opener bids a "waiting" 3♣ to start cuebidding lower.

Responder would actually have two good options here. He could bid 4♦ as a splinter, knowing that Opener will place him with better than the spade King and heart Queen, for instance. Or, he could cue 3♦ as a control and take it forward.

After the splinter, Opener is not impressed. He needs three Kings to not have this slam be on a hook, and a splinter with all three side Kings and a stiff diamond is a bit of an underbid. He could take one last stab by bidding 4♥, which Responder might raise to 5♥ (an overbid, perhaps), but he will then know that this hand turns on a club hook, which is 50-50, plus no problems in any suit, which makes the slam anti-percentage.

After the 3♦ cue option, Opener continues with a 3♥ cue. Responder then simply cues 4♥. Again, Opener, this time more rapidly, knows that Responder does not have the club King. Furthermore, holding the spade King, heart King, and diamond Ace, Responder would surely show serious slam interest by bidding 3NT. But, if Opener again is aggressive (crazy) and asks for Aces, that will be cleared up and a nice stop at 5♠ should result.

Of course, anyone can opt to bid an anti-percentage slam anyway because he expects the opponents to bid an anti-percentage slam and wants to avoid a swing, if a swing would be bad. For me, against the Katz, Cayne, Nickell, or Diamond teams, I would want and probably desperately need that swing. In any event, it seems better to make an informed decision than a guess, and the informed decision is easy on this hand because cuebidding started after trumps were agreed at the two-level.

A quick one from the 2008 World Mind Sports Games in Beijing:

Opener: ♠ A J 10 3 ♥ A Q J 9 ♦ K Q J ♣ A 5
Responder: ♠ Q 8 7 4 ♥ K 4 2 ♦ 7 4 3 ♣ K 8 3

The Italian auction was reasonable. Opener started with 2♣, heard 2♦ waiting, and rebid 2NT. A Puppet Stayman sequence resulted in all suits bid at the three-level, three of them artificially, to agree spades with Opener's 3♠ call. Two more calls and a signoff.

With our approach, Opener starts with 2♦, and Responder immediately sets trumps and shows some reasonable values by bidding 2NT. Opener bids a waiting 3♣ to start the cuebidding up, and we eventually end up at the same contract, unless someone gets excited and hopes for a successful spade finesse (which failed in practice).

How much nicer is it to agree spades immediately and to start cuebidding at such a low level rather than to spend time making seven bids to just set trumps?

Another one from Beijing shows how our 2♦ opening bid helps with the troubling 4-4-4-1 hands while also showing the value of the weak raise of spades.

Opener: ♠ A K J 4 ♥ Q ♦ A Q 8 4 ♣ A J 6 3
Responder: ♠ 10 9 7 5 ♥ 8 2 ♦ K 7 6 5 ♣ 9 8 5

Opening this hand with a standard 2♣ is troubling, because 4441 hands are so difficult. Many would probably downgrade the stiff heart Queen and just open 1♦. Even using our approach, that may be the best course of action.

However, suppose that Opener feels aggressive today. He is less troubled opening this 2♦ because he will put his spades on the table immediately. If spades cannot immediately be agreed, he may well opt to rebid 3♣ as a convenient call. Although that implies longer clubs, we know that the 4-1-4-4 and 4-4-1-4 alternatives are possible. So, considering all of this, our brave Opener tries a 2♦ opening.

Responder can now slow the auction down with a 3♥ call. This, again, is a transfer to 3♠ and shows either a bust hand or a minimum game raise.

Opener, who clearly has a minimum, suggests the signoff by bidding only 3♠ – he would bid 4♠ with extras or even pursue slam with a monster.

Responder raises 3♠ to 4♠ because of his diamond King, and the doubleton as a bonus. Now we need some luck.

Another from Beijing:

Opener: ♠ A Q 4 3   ♥ A Q 9 2   ♦ A K 10   ♣ K 4
Responder: ♠ K 9 8 7 5   ♥ J 8   ♦ Q 8 7 6   ♣ A 9

The standard auction is a 2♣ opening, 2♦ waiting, 2NT as 22-23 balanced, a transfer, and a decision as to whether the hand merits a super-acceptance, followed by a decision as to which way to super-accept best.

Our auction starts with 2♦, which allows Responder to immediately set trumps (2NT) and Opener to immediately start the cuebidding up with the waiting 3♣ call. Easy, fewer bids, less space burned finding fit. These are all great things to experience.

It is a shame Opener did not have the golden
♠ A Q J 3 ♥ Q 9 ♦ A K J 2 ♣ K Q J, eh?

You see that a lot of real world sequences start
out with the 2♦ opening, positive spade agreement 2NT,
and the waiting 3♣ call. However, this is not always the
case.

Consider the following situation, also from
Beijing:

Opener: ♠ A K J 7 6 ♥ A K Q ♦ -- ♣ K J 9 7 3
Responder: ♠ 10 5 3 2 ♥ J 9 6 ♦ K Q 9 ♣ Q 8 6

After a 2♦ Opening, Opener hears a 2NT
response, immediately showing spade support and a
promising hand. With only three losers, and a known
nine-card spade fit, Opener is very excited.

He could opt to just bid a waiting 3♣ to start a
cuebidding sequence. Responder would bid an
uninteresting 3♦. Opener would continue with 3♥ and
hear a signoff. That would not help much.

Alternatively, and a better move, would be for
Opener to show his club suit by bidding 3♠, showing a
club second suit and ideally in the way where Opener
shows two of the top three spades as well (3NT being
used to show clubs but lesser spades). That seems
perfect, as it enables Responder to cuebid the club
Queen, a critical card.

That makes for a nice sequence. Recognizing
that the diamond King and Queen may not be worth as
much opposite a black two-suiter, Responder can bid a
non-serious 4♣, showing the club Queen. Opener can
now visualize the play fairly well. With that club 9 as a
bonus, it sure seems that clubs will play for only one
loser fairly reliably. With at least nine combined spades,

the odds seem to favor spades coming in more often than not for no losers. So, 6♠ seems odds on, regardless of which club Responder has. Opener, therefore, could probably just blast 6♠.

Should opener be cautious, he could simply ask for Aces with a RKCB 4NT call, to get to the issue of the spade Queen. Or, he could continue to cuebid. He could even bid 5♦ as Exclusion RKCB.

Unfortunately, the Queen-third of spades was behind, in the real world. Not all good bidding is rewarded.

When Responder has Fewer than Four Spades

Auctions work well when an immediate fit is found. Sometimes that is not the case because Responder has fewer than four spades. However, even that bit of information provides valuable impact upon the options for the partnership. When Opener can show that he has only four spades, that response by Responder denying four spades allows a spade bid later in the auction to be freed up for artificial raises, artificial forcing bids, and the like.

Responder has many options when he lacks four spades. Again, his basic structure depends upon his basic hand type. Opener also will be able to describe much about his hand after Responder's call. Most of the time, however, Responder will bid a waiting and artificial 2♥ call, much like the artificial and waiting 2♥ call often used over a standard 2♣ opening, with the difference being that the standard 2♥ response is negative about *overall strength* whereas our 2♥ waiting response to the 2♦ opening is negative about *spade length*. As this is the most common response, it makes sense to describe generally Opener's usual options.

If Opener has a balanced hand with four or five spades, he will rebid 2NT. Because Opener has already promised four spades, he will be known to have four or five spades with that balanced hand, reducing his potential heart length accordingly. As Responder has also already denied four spades, he will have fewer possible tasks to perform in the majors himself. This will provide superior options and more room for Responder, enabled by Opener's potential pattern limitations in the majors. As a simple example, note that a transfer to spades would make no sense, as Responder has already denied a spade suit, freeing up a 3♥ call for some other purpose.

If Opener has an unbalanced hand with five or more spades, he will rebid a normal-looking 2♠, with the remaining auction parallel to standard sequences after either a strong 2♠ opening or a 2♣ opening, a 2♦ waiting response, and a 2♠ rebid. As our waiting 2♥ response said nothing about general strength, however, you may want to use some form of second negative call. Note that there is no functional difference between the standard auction 2♣ - P - 2♦(waiting) - P - 2♠ and our auction 2♦ - P - 2♥ - P - 2♠. The end result is exactly the same.

If Opener's hand pattern was a spade canapé hand, meaning a hand with four spades and a longer second suit, he will complete his pattern by rebidding in his second suit. Because this call will eliminate spades as a possible strain, spade calls can be used artificially to save space. As a simple example, consider the auction 2♦ - P - 2♥ - P - 3♣. Responder would normally be required to bid 4♣ to raise clubs. We, however, have no need for a natural 3♠ in this sequence, allowing Responder to raise clubs by bidding 3♠ when he does not want to bypass 3NT. On the appropriate hand, he can still bid an immediate 4♣, however. But, he will now have two options.[8]

When Opener has 4441 pattern, with any stiff (except spades, of course), he can handle these difficult hands the traditional way, by bidding these hands as if they were strong, balanced hands. However, we actually have some chance of Opener describing this difficult pattern because of our enhanced approach. He will also have the ability to make a jump to show some of these hand types immediately.

All of this is explained next.

---

[8] These auctions will be similar, in principle, to the auction where Opener opens 1♥, Responder responds with a forcing 1NT, and Opener rebids a minor, like 2♣. Responder would never bid 2♠ as natural, because he already denied spades by not responding 1♠ the first time. Opener clearly does not have five spades for this sequence. Therefore, because the spade suit has been eliminated as a possible strain, 2♠ by Responder, called the "Impossible 2♠," shows support for Opener's minor and a different hand than would be shown had Responder just bid 3♣. Think of the 3♠ call in our sequence as an "Impossible 3♠" call.

After the Waiting Two Heart Response, Denying Four Spades

Opener bids <u>Two No Trump</u> with a Balanced Hand and Four or Five Spades

Opener bids <u>Two Spades</u> with Five or More Spades in an Unbalanced Hand

Opener bids a New Suit with Four Spades and 5+ in the Second Suit

2♦-P-2♥-P-3♣ with 4 Spades and 5 or More Clubs

2♦-P-2♥-P-3♦ with 4 Spades and 5 or More Diamonds

2♦-P-2♥-P-3♥ with 4 Spades and 5 or More Hearts

Opener can bid 2NT with 4441 and Any Stiff (Except Spades)

Optional Treatments:

2♦-P-2♥-P-3NT with 4♥/4♠ and 4-5♦

2♦-P-2♥-P-4♣ with 4♥/4♠ and 4-5♦ (too strong for 3NT)

2♦-P-2♥-P-3♠ with 4♠ and 4-4, 4-5, or 5-4 in the minors

2♦-P-2♥-P-3♣ could be 4-4-1-4 or 4-4-0-5

The Artificial Two Hearts Waiting Response

Unless Responder has a positive response in his own suit, he will usually respond Two Hearts to show fewer than four spades. His strength is unknown at this point, as the only immediate negative available is the Three Hearts transfer acceptance of spades. So, a Two Hearts response could be based upon a very weak hand. Or, Responder might have anything else. He just does not have four or more spades.

After a Two Hearts response, Opener has many normal-looking options. Some of the meanings may sound unusual, especially if you are unfamiliar with canapé bidding. However, the simple canapé bidding will be picked up quite easily.

Spades as the Longest Suit

First, Opener could rebid Two Spades. This auction reverts back to standard, except that we all know that Responder cannot have *four-card* support. If you think about it, other than the first two bids being technically different, there is nothing functionally different between a 2♣ opening bid (standard), a waiting 2♦ response (one that does not establish a game force), and a 2♠ rebid (promising five or more spades), and our sequence, which also ends up at the level of 2♠ with the same information exchanged. The sole difference is that we have the slight advantage of knowing that Responder will not have four spades with Opener.

When we start with this sequence, Opener's spades will be his longest suit, or he may have two suits of the same length (5-5, for example). The one slightly important note here is that Opener will rebid 2♠ with five or more spades and four hearts. Later, we will discuss sequences where Opener shows four hearts and a longer minor. You might wonder about four hearts and a longer spade suit during that discussion, but remember that we just bid spades first with that holding.

Whatever you would normally play here, after a 2♣ opening and a 2♠ rebid, works. Maybe 2NT is a second negative. Maybe 3♣ is the second negative. Maybe you are an optimist and you have no second negative. Whatever works for you is fine. Now, admittedly this sequence is inferior to an auction where 2♣-P-2♦-P-2♠ would have been game forcing (because 2♦ was a waiting bid and game-forcing) or where 2♣-P-2♥-P-2♠ would be tailored by a 2♥ double negative response. I will accept that criticism, in exchange for everything else that I gain.

Also, Opener might jump to 3♠ to set trumps and to demand cuebidding, as is normal practice. Again, this suffers from some loss when the 2♦ Opening is used as contrasted with the game forcing 2♦ or double negative 2♥ responses to a normal 2♣ opening. Our Opener will not know Responder's strength, which could be dead bust.

Minor-Spade Canapé Bids

Suppose, however, that Opener has four spades and a longer minor. With standard methods, Opener would have been forced to open one of the minor (and possibly hear a pass-out) or would have to rebid three of a minor after Responder's bid in response to 2♣. That call would create problems. After 3♣, Responder could not raise clubs without bypassing 3NT. With a five-card major, Responder could bid it. With a four-card major, Responder would probably bid an artificial 3♦, waiting to hear if Opener could rebid in a major. If Responder held both majors, life would be even more complicated.

What if Opener's minor is diamonds? A 3♦ rebid would leave no room to work out the majors. One solution was suggested by Giorgio Belladonna, namely that Opener's jumps to 3♥ or 3♠ would show four of that major and longer diamonds, but that is quite a preemptive solution, and it deprives the partnership of the trump-setting jumps. Further, no suit could be agreed below 3NT. Also, if Opener has specifically 4-3-6-0 and Responder something like 3-5-1-4 shape, the heart fit is lost, or at least very difficult to find.

Look how nicely our new approach handles the spade-minor canapé hands, however. With five or more of a minor (not as much need for a six-card suit here) and four spades, Opener rebids in his minor. He has already shown the four-card spade suit, so his picture is much more complete already.

Sure, we are now in that scary world of canapé bidding. But, is that such a difficult concept here? Opener showed four spades but was greeted by a partner who could not support his spades. Now, Opener is simply bidding his long suit. The fact that this sequence happens to be a canapé sequence (bidding your short suit before your long suit) does not make this all that mysterious, does it?

After a minor rebid, Responder has many tools available to him. Because a spade fit has been ruled out, a 3♠ call is available to support the minor. Note, however, that Responder might "support the minor" as a waiting bid of sorts, to avoid bidding 3NT himself. This "support call" is therefore somewhat all-purpose. With slam interest and good support for the minor, Responder would just skip over 3NT and bid raise Opener's minor to the four-level. However, with no real slam interest, a 3♠ call might be used to encourage a 3NT call, or to offer a substitution for a "second negative" call in response to a minor rebid (Responder bids 3♠ and then passes after any 3NT call or any rebid of Opener's minor, or rebids Opener's minor as cheaply as possible otherwise). Responder might even bid 3♠ with slam interest, if his minor support is marginal.

Thus, consider a typical auction:

2♦	P	2♥	P
3♣	P	3♠	P
?			

Opener showed four spades when he opened 2♦. Responder denied four spades by bidding 2♥. Opener showed 5+ clubs by bidding 3♣, and also showed that he started with exactly four spades. No spade fit is possible. This allows Responder to bid 3♠ to show club support, below 3NT. Opener could, therefore, return to 3NT to suggest a hand with four spades, five clubs, and not enough to go past 3NT, or with any hand where Opener thinks that 3NT is probably the best contract. If Responder wants to move on, he can. But, the partnership may stop at 3NT if that is best.

If Responder had slam interest, he probably would have opted to bid an immediate 4♣ over Opener's 3♣ call. If Responder instead bids 3♠, he might have a weak hand, with which he will pass if Opener rebids 4♣ and with which he may bid a non-forcing 4♣ call over Opener's 3NT call.

Responder also can bid a five-card heart suit in this sequence if he desires. Responder is not much interested in bidding a four-card heart suit, as Opener is unlikely to have specifically 4-4-0-5 pattern (or 4-4-5-0 pattern after a 3♦ call). Thus, after Opener rebids 3♣ or 3♦, Responder can bid 3♥ as a natural call, showing five or more hearts (but not the right hand for an immediate positive bid in hearts).

If Opener bids 3♣, Responder might also bid 3♦ as a waiting bid just to see if Opener bids 3♥ to show 4-4-0-5 pattern. For this reason, the 3♦ call is not strictly a call that shows a diamond suit. If Opener has 4-4-0-5 pattern, he can bid 3♥ over Responder's 3♦ call and complete his pattern. Who else can do that?

As an aside, Opener *might* opt to show a false canapé by bidding 3♣ with 4-4-1-4 shape if he thinks that this is a superior way to bid the hand tactically, hoping for a 3♦ call from Responder after which he can bid 3♥.

The canapé approach to handling hands with a four-card major and a longer minor is probably somewhat familiar. A lot of folks play that after a standard 2♣ opening, and a waiting 2♦ response, Opener can leap to 3♥ or 3♠ to show that major and longer diamonds.

Our methods work better, however. First of all, we can find the spade fit immediately. Second, we can handle either minor being longer than the major. Third, we can eliminate the major as a possible fit, which saves space.

Consider an actual deal from the 2008 World Mind Sports Games in Beijing where this issue came up.

Opener: ♠ A Q 9 4 ♥ J ♦ A K Q J 6 3 ♣ A 9
Responder: ♠ 10 8 6 ♥ A Q 9 7 ♦ 9 8 7 ♣ Q 8 6

In the "standard" method of showing a strong canapé with spades and diamonds, as used in practice by South Africa in Beijing, Opener started 2♣, Responder bid 2♦ (waiting), and Opener bid 3♠. Responder then bid 4♦, and a slam was reached. With both missing key spades protected and behind the Ace-Queen, with the heart King protected and behind the Ace-Queen, and with the King of clubs over the Queen, the only good news was that diamonds split 2-2. Obviously, the slam is hopeless. But, there was insufficient space to work that out in time.

Our auction is better. After a 2♦ start to show the four spades, Responder immediately throws that suit out of the picture by bidding 2♥, waiting without four spades. Opener then bids 3♦, which places us at the same level as the South Africans. However, because we have eliminated spades as a possible strain, Responder can satisfy his need to show diamond support below 3NT by bidding 3♠.

Now, 3♠ might be an overbid, but it is less so than 4♦ and gives the partnership room to unwind the auction. Also, it is true that Opener might overreact to the 3♠ support bid, but he is not sort of forced into the slam movement simply by the dread of partner having bypassed 3NT. I'm sure that you can see the merits of being able to mention diamond interest without bypassing 3NT.

Handling the Specific 4-4-4-1 and 4-4-5-0 hands

If you are concerned about missing the 4-4 heart fit when Opener holds 4-4-5-0 pattern, then I can suggest a treatment. Opener can jump to 3NT after Responder's 2♥ call as a conventional bid, promising 4-4-4-1 or 4-4-5-0 pattern. A jump to 4♣ after the 2♥ response shows the same pattern with a hand that is too strong for 3NT, which is non-forcing. Thus, this 4♣ jump rebid is somewhat like a splinter without any fit yet being decided. 3NT, instead, shows the same pattern but without sufficient strength to bypass 3NT.

If Opener does bid 3NT, I like to use the relay to show a weak hand. Thus, Responder can bid 4♣ as a relay to 4♦, after which Responder might pass, bid 4♥, bid 4♠ to play in the Moysian fit, or bid a very discouraging and semi-gambling 5♦. With extra stuff, Responder can raise the diamonds naturally by bidding a forcing 4♦, bid 4♥ as a non-forcing but slam-invitational heart preference bid, bid 4♠ (the out-of-focus major) as RKCB for diamonds, or bid 4NT as RKCB for hearts.

If Opener instead bids the power 4♣ "splinter," I think that 4♦ should be the weak relay (again, possibly to play in 4♠ or even in 4NT). An immediate 4♥ or 5♦ would be encouraging but non-forcing, and 4♠/4NT RKCB bids as over the 3NT option.

Some Hands Featuring a Canapé Minor Rebid

A nice deal from the 2005 Bermuda Bowl in Estoril illustrates well the merits of this opening even when Responder does not have a spade fit but Opener makes a minor canapé rebid. Consider the deal:

```
            ♠ A K 5 3
            ♥ K Q 4
            ♦ A K Q 3 2
            ♣ 2

♠ 8 6 4                      ♠ Q 10 9 2
♥ A 9 8 3                    ♥ 10 6 5 2
♦ 8 6                        ♦ J
♣ A K 9 6                    ♣ Q J 8 7

            ♠ J 7
            ♥ J 7
            ♦ 10 9 7 5 4
            ♣ 10 5 4 3
```

North is in fourth seat and hears three passes. As we know, a strong 2♣ opening for standard systems cannot easily handle this pattern. Accordingly, the practical solution may be a 1♦ opening. But, as can be seen, South should probably pass this, which would result in a likely pass-out and a diamond game missed.

For us, the ability to handle this pattern makes life better. North can open 2♦, comfortable that strain selection will not be a problem. South, lacking anything redeeming and also lacking a spade fit, bids a waiting 2♥. North now completes his pattern by bidding 3♦, a call that does not preempt North-South from finding a possible heart fit had South held five or more hearts. South has a terrible hand, but the five-card support in diamonds, plus two doubletons and what might be a useful spade Jack, is just enough to try 5♦, a rewarded bid. If South is a pessimist, he can bid 3♠, instead, which is artificial and shows some sort of diamond support, planning to correct 3NT to 4♦, non-forcing.

Another interesting deal, this time from the 2008 European Bridge Team Championships, is worth considering as well:

```
              ♠ 7
              ♥ A 10 8 5 2
              ♦ 8 5
              ♣ K Q 6 3 2

♠ K 6 4                        ♠ A J 9 3
♥ 9 6                          ♥ K Q 3
♦ 9 7 6 4 2                    ♦ A K Q J 3
♣ J 9 8                        ♣ 7

              ♠ Q 10 8 5 2
              ♥ J 7 4
              ♦ 10
              ♣ A 10 5 4
```

First seat, East has two options. The obvious option is to open 1♦, planning to later jump shift in spades to establish a game force. No one using normal methods would consider opening 2♣, because the rebid disaster is obvious.

However, consider the problem with our tools. With all of the honors working, and a very nice spade 9, East has good reason to consider a 2♦ opening, especially considering how easy the rebid situation will become. If Responder does have a spade fit, we find that immediately, with a spade game probably making opposite as little as one more spade from West and the actual hand that he has, with which he might very well pass 1♦. If Responder does not have a spade fit, as is actually the case, Opener, after 2♦ - P - 2♥ as the start that actually will occur, can rebid 3♦ without fear of losing the heart suit, and with the comfort of having shown nine of his cards.

In practice, this sequence surely leads our East-West to the ideal 5♦ contract, and we have no moments of discomfort. Responder can place the contract immediately in 5♦ by jumping over 3♦. Alternatively, Responder might like his spade King with five-card diamond support, and he might therefore show extremely slight slam interest by bidding a waiting and support-showing 3♠ before correcting a possible 3NT call to 5♦.

On the next deal, from the 2008 United States Bridge Championship, East will get to support diamonds below 3NT, which is critical:

          ♠ J 10 9
          ♥ A 6 3 2
          ♦ 10 5 4
          ♣ K 8 5

♠ A K Q 8   ♠ 3 2
♥ K   ♥ J 9 8 7
♦ A K Q J 3   ♦ 9 7 2
♣ Q 10 9   ♣ J 7 6 3

          ♠ 7 6 5 4
          ♥ Q 10 5 4
          ♦ 8 6
          ♣ A 4 2

West deals and opens 2♦, showing four or more spades. East, who lacks four spades, declines spades by bidding an otherwise waiting 2♥. West completes his pattern by bidding 3♦, showing exactly four spades and five or more diamonds.

What is East supposed to do with that? He has utter junk and nowhere to go. However, because he has already denied four spades, and because Opener has just denied holding five spades himself (a canapé rebid promises exactly four spades), East can show support for the diamonds (he does have a fit. technically) by bidding 3♠. This is nice, as it is below 3NT.

West should bid his own hand and let East show interest himself if he has the right cards for a slam. West needs a lot for a diamond slam. With his pattern already shown and so much in the two remaining suits, 3NT looks like the practical and rewarded call.

Heart-Spade Canapé Hands:

The same basic approach works when Opener holds four spades and five or more hearts. After a Two Hearts response (denying four spades), Opener rebids Three Hearts. If Responder wants to agree hearts, he can cuebid at the four-level or sign off at 4♥. 3NT declines hearts. I believe that allowing Responder to distinguish how strong his heart support may be by either cuebidding or not cuebidding is more important in these sequences than showing a minor or minors. Incidentally, however, this problem may justify an aggressive use of minor positives by Responder earlier if he has fewer than four spades and extreme shortness (stiff or void) in hearts.

Note that Responder's 2♥ relay response did steal the contract from Opener. On many auctions, we will be able to right-side contracts that others cannot right-side. In this sequence, we lose. However, do not forget that Responder bid hearts already. There is no sense using delayed transfers now.

You will want to use 3♠ as a "hesitant" call, implying a two-card heart suit. Unlike after minor canapé rebids, where 3♠ showed support for the minor, here we will use 3♠ to show general uncertainty as to strain. Responder will likely have two hearts for this call. This also offers a better solution when Opener has four spades and *six* hearts, as Opener rebidding the hearts at the four-level might be unwise if he catches Responder with a stiff or void in hearts.

One observation that you may have at this point is that this heart canapé rebid may leave us at a very higher level opposite a Responder who may have utter trash with no fit and no good options. While this is true, this deficit to the approach is not that bad in context.

First of all, if Responder does have that death hand, much of the rest of the field will probably have the same dreadful auction after a 2♣ opening and a 2♥ negative response, followed by the same 3♥ rebid by Opener. However, they will not have the tool of a waiting "punt" 3♠ call, needing that call to actually show spades. Plus, we will actually be better off in these situations when Responder does have spade support and showed it earlier with a 3♥ weak transfer to spades. We beat the field which does not yet know about the spade fit and cannot possibly stop on a dime at 3♠ with a 4-4 fit. They might not even find the spade fit.

You recall how the immediacy of the raise of the spade suit allows canapé hands to be bid better earlier. A deal in Shanghai shows us how much more effectively the heart-spade canapé deals can be handled.

The deal:

```
              ♠ A 9 6 4
              ♥ A K 10 9 7
              ♦ A Q 6
              ♣ A

♠ K 8 7 2                    ♠ J 10 5 3
♥ 4 2                        ♥ 6 5 3
♦ K 5 3                      ♦ 9 2
♣ Q 9 8 5                    ♣ K 10 7 2

              ♠ Q
              ♥ Q J 8
              ♦ J 10 8 7 4
              ♣ J 6 4 3
```

In standard methods, the North hand presents a serious problem. If you open 2♣ and hear a double negative 2♥ response, a 3♥ rebid is ugly. Not only does it force game without sufficient assets to merit that action, but it also jams spade-suit exploration. If Responder must have five spades to bid them over 3♥, the possible 4-4 fit will be lost. Thus, this auction will probably get too high and in the wrong strain if you open 2♣ using standard methods. As a result, there were a lot of 1♥ openings.

Our methods work wonders. By opening 2♦, North immediately puts the spade suit on the table. Had South held four (or more) spades, the strain problem would be solved, with plenty of space to cuebid. However, this time South lacks spade support and accordingly bids 2♥, waiting. Now, I'll grant that this does force Opener to bid 3♥ as before. However, our 3♥ call shows a heart-spade canapé and, because more description is provided, at least *strain* will not be a problem. We even have the ability for Responder, had he held only two hearts, to show partial support (by bidding 3♠, which cannot be our fit) in case Opener were holding 6♥/4♠.

That principle could have been effectively implemented on a problem deal from the 2006 World Pairs Championship. The deal:

```
              ♠ 10 5 4
              ♥ J 5
              ♦ Q J 2
              ♣ A J 7 5 4

 ♠ Q 6 3                      ♠ A 9 8
 ♥ 4 2                        ♥ 10 9 7
 ♦ 9 8 7 5 3                  ♦ 6 4
 ♣ 10 8 6                     ♣ K Q 9 3 2

              ♠ K J 7 2
              ♥ A K Q 8 6 3
              ♦ A K 10
              ♣ ---
```

South opens 2♦ in second seat, promising four or more spades. North lacks four spades and has no suit worthy of a positive response. Had North held a stiff heart instead, and a sixth club, he might have made an aggressive 3♣ response to the 2♦ opening, as a prepared bid, especially if his diamonds were weaker. With a doubleton heart, however, North has no problems.

Accordingly, North bids a waiting 2♥. South shows the heart-spade canapé by bidding 3♥. Again, the fact that this series of calls eliminates the spade suit as a possible strain allows North to bid 3♠ to imply the doubleton heart. That gets us to 4♥ without the need for South to demand a heart strain, which would have been a bad idea if North had held a void in hearts.

The hesitant 3♠ call can also be illustrated with a deal from the 2007 United States Bridge Championship:

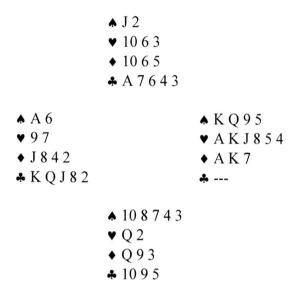

```
              ♠ J 2
              ♥ 10 6 3
              ♦ 10 6 5
              ♣ A 7 6 4 3

♠ A 6                          ♠ K Q 9 5
♥ 9 7                          ♥ A K J 8 5 4
♦ J 8 4 2                      ♦ A K 7
♣ K Q J 8 2                    ♣ ---

              ♠ 10 8 7 4 3
              ♥ Q 2
              ♦ Q 9 3
              ♣ 10 9 5
```

After North deals and passes, West has the first decision. With only 20 HCP, many would just open 1♥, especially with only a 2♣ opening for strong hands. That may be the best call anyway. Give East a little more body, something like ♠ K Q 10 9 ♥ A K J 10 8 5 ♦ A K 7 ♣ ---, and a 2♦ bid has a lot of merit, for the obvious reason that this looks like a fairly pure three-loser hand. But, to carry on the story, let us pretend that East has that hand or that East wants to be aggressive with this holding. He opens 2♦.

West has good cause to consider a 3♣ positive response, with that nice club suit. Maybe he should have a sixth club, but 3♣ takes up so little space and is quite descriptive with this hand. This option would make a lot of sense with one less heart and one more spade. The auction is really easy after the more reserved 2♥ response and 3♠ rebid by Responder, but let's assume that West is aggressive as well and makes that positive call in clubs, just to show how easily this auction proceeds. Either way, West has denied four spades.

East also has an easy rebid after a positive 3♣ response. He completes his canapé pattern by bidding 3♥. Notice that East would have to bid 3♠ after 3♣ with five spades and four hearts, which is a reason for West not to bid 3♣ if he has four hearts. But with this major pattern West could care less about a four-card heart suit, or a five-card spade suit for that matter. Notice also that this 3♥ call, whether after a 3♣ call or a waiting 2♥ call, still shows a heart-spade canapé with exactly four spades and five or more hearts. East could jump to 4♥ with the freak hand of five spades and six hearts (as you will soon learn).

West now has a nice rebid after this 3♥ call, the same call whether he had started with 3♣ or with the more reserved 2♥ waiting option. With ugly diamonds and a doubleton heart, he makes the "punt" bid of 3♠, which is possible because Opener has limited his spades to a four-card suit and Responder has already denied a fit.

Opener can accept hearts now. Whether East decides to let West consider the slam on his own (bidding a passable 4♥) or decides to show slam interest is up to East and his continuing state of mind. If he does want to indicate slam interest, what should he do? It seems fairly straightforward that 3NT would be to play and that 4♣ would show delayed club support, probably with 4-5-1-3 shape. 4♥ would also be to play. But, what about 4♦? That call seems to be a power acceptance of hearts, in my view. I cannot imagine any other interpretation. Had Responder's suit been diamonds, I would take 4♣ as the power acceptance of hearts in this sequence. Of course, you could agree to play that 4♣ always shows support for Responder's minor and that 4♦ always shows a power acceptance of hearts, as flags, if you want.

If Responder had bid 2♥ initially, where there was no minor suit in focus, then perhaps this 3♠ call creates a problem for Opener. But then I think that the minor calls should be either natural fragment bids (if you use a strictly natural approach) or shortness bids (if you prefer the Kokish theory here), accepting the heart invite, as you and your partner agree.

Freak Two-Suiters

As we have already discussed, a 3NT call after a 2♥ spade-declining response shows a hand with 4-4-5-0 or 4-4-4-1 pattern and a 4♣ call shows 4-4-5-0 or 4-4-4-1 pattern with extras, as these are two "troubling" patterns. This leaves three other rebids worth discussing, namely 4♦, 4♥, and 4♠.

These calls each show 6-5 two-suiters with six of the second suit and five spades, a "super canapé" holding, 4♠ showing clubs as the second suit. This purifies a 2♠ rebid as a bid that always shows equal or longer spades, even when Opener shows a two-suited hand. As the 5-6 canapé two-suiter rebid is a fairly well-defined bid, and fairly impossible to describe at all using normal techniques, I'm will not even bother to explain what to do next. You figure it out! Generally, though, I'd expect a hand with about two losers and bid accordingly. It is difficult to construct a 5-6 hand with three losers that should be opened with a 2♦ opening.

This treatment would have helped in a deal from the 2008 European Bridge Team Championship:

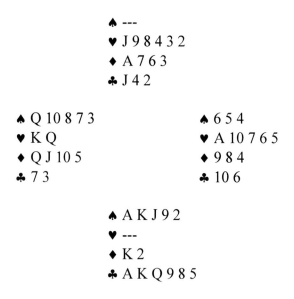

♠ ---
♥ J 9 8 4 3 2
♦ A 7 6 3
♣ J 4 2

♠ Q 10 8 7 3   ♠ 6 5 4
♥ K Q   ♥ A 10 7 6 5
♦ Q J 10 5   ♦ 9 8 4
♣ 7 3   ♣ 10 6

♠ A K J 9 2
♥ ---
♦ K 2
♣ A K Q 9 8 5

South opens 2♦ in first seat, promising four or more spades. North lacks four spades and has no suit worthy of a positive, and accordingly he bids a waiting 2♥. South now jumps to 4♠ to show the Super-Canapé with five spades and longer clubs. Remember, he must jump in spades to show the club suit because 4♣ is used for another meaning.

Back to North. That diamond Ace seems to have a good chance of working, as Opener is not likely to be void in diamonds when North is looking at six hearts and has good reason to believe that the void, if any, is probably in hearts, although nothing is clear. The third club looks nice, as well. However, North really dislikes that spade void. A stiff Jack of spades, even, would look a lot better. A fourth club would also be much more appealing with the void in spades. Sure, to get to a hand with high-card points worthy of a 2♦ opening with 6-5 shape, South likely has about a two-loser hand, but the dubious diamond value, the lack of a fourth club, and that troubling spade void probably should convince North to sign off at 5♣.

As it turns out, 6♣ happens to make, and the grand makes on any lead except a club. Perhaps North should be more aggressive. Had North held East's diamond 9, the grand would be cold on any lead.

One Possible Optional Treatment

If you have been thinking through the patterns possible for Opener, you may realize that one pattern is not handled well. With 4-4-4-1 or 4-4-5-0 pattern, Opener can rebid 3NT, or 4♣ with a very strong hand. With 4-4-0-5, Opener can rebid 3♣ and then show his hearts if Responder bids 3♦. With 4-4-1-4 hands, Opener can select between a tactical 3♣ "lie" and treating the hand as balanced.

However, one difficult pattern type is 4-1-4-4, as well as 4-0-4-5 or 4-0-5-4 if you want to focus both minors. A possible alternative solution for these hands is to give up the jump rebid in spades after a 2♥ waiting call. Instead, 3♠ would show this hand type. You could still opt to treat some of these hands as balanced if the hand seems to call for that solution, of course.

Using this approach, Responder is expected to bid 3NT or to pick a minor. My suggestion would be for a four-level call in a minor (4♣ or 4♦) to be passable. With enough for a minor game, but barely, Responder could jump to 5♣ or 5♦. With extra stuff and a minor fit, Responder could flag his minor fit, meaning 4♥ for clubs and 4♠ for diamonds. Responder might also bid a Quantitative 4NT.

The use of this optional treatment would complete a package of options for handling 4441 hands.

With these hands, you could, for good cause, treat them as balanced.

However, if you have 4-4-4-1 or 4-4-5-0 (short club), your option will be to open 2♦ and then rebid either 4♣ with a big hand or 3NT with less enthusiasm, perhaps thought of as splintering in the short suit. If you have 4-4-1-4 or 4-4-0-5, your option will be a 3♣ rebid, because that allows a 3♦ asking bid. If your hand is 4-1-4-4, 4-0-5-4, or 4-0-4-5, you can open 2♦ to show the four-card spade suit and then rebid your longer minor if that looks right (with the void), rebid the hand as if balanced with 4-1-4-4 if that looks right, or rebid 3♠. That bid shows both minors just like a 2♣ opening followed by a 3♠ rebid, as you will soon see. With 1-4-4-4, 0-4-5-4, or 0-4-4-5, you also will be able to have these three options, albeit through a 2♣ opening and a 2♠ rebid, as you will also see.

Thus, these three-suited hands will be easily handled.

Balanced Hands

The handling of balanced hands is interesting. For practical reasons, however, that discussion will be handled separately. Suffice it to say for now that a 2NT rebid by Opener after a Two Hearts response shows a balanced hand, with four or five spades. The responses thereto will be discussed in a later section.

The Positive Responses

Just as with other methods, Responder may have a "positive response." This is often defined as showing a five-card suit with fewer than seven losers. Maybe suit quality is part of your agreement. Whatever you use is fine. However, remember that minor-suit positive responses tend to deny four hearts. Further, remember that minor-suit positives also are aggressively bid if Responder has a stiff heart and the other minor looks ugly for 3NT purposes.

There are two changes to system because of the Two Diamonds opening, one a minor change and one a major change.

The minor "change" is that a positive response in a minor (3♣ or 3♦) or in hearts (2♠ will be the positive bid in hearts) denies a four-card spade suit. That is probably not earth-shattering.

The major change is the strange call for the heart positive. Because 2♥ is the waiting response, we need something else for a heart positive. My solution is that 2♠ shows the heart positive.

Also, you may have noticed that there is no defined meaning for a 3♠ response. I would play that as showing a limited positive response with both minors and shortness (stiff or void) in spades. The positive is "limited" as showing something like 5-8 HCP. Something like ♠ x ♥ x x ♦ K 10 x x x ♣ K x x x x might be an average hand.

As an example of this 3♠ call for the minors, consider a deal from the 2008 World Mind Sports Games in Beijing.

Opener: ♠ A K Q 5 2 ♥ A 8 2 ♦ K ♣ A K 8 2
Responder: ♠ 4 ♥ K 5 ♦ A J 9 8 2 ♣ 10 7 5 4 3

The results for the match between USA and Germany were plain odd. Germany shot really low, and chose a strange strain, declaring 4♠. USA saw stars and went for all 13 tricks at 7NT, not even using the ruffing value.

How about this. Opener starts 2♦, strong with spades. Responder, having a stiff spade, both minors, and about the right range, bids the artificial 3♠ to show his minor two-suiter.

Opener will now evaluate the diamond King for what it really is worth, both as an honor and as a ruffing value because of the fourth club. The majors seem locked up. So, from Opener's perspective, the sole issue is whether Responder does or does not have the trump Queen.

4♣, which sets trumps, should probably be used in this sequence as an immediate RKCB call, because Responder's shape is already so well defined. Alternatively, 4♣ could set trumps and cuebidding could start. Either way, Opener will sooner or later find out that the club Queen is missing and will settle for the practical 6♣.

Positive Responses

Three Clubs or Three Diamonds Natural, Not Four Spades

Two Spades Artificial Positive in Hearts, Not Four Spades

Three Spades as Minor Two Suiter, Limited

74

Extra Discussion of the 2♠ Heart Positive

Again, we use a 2♠ response to a 2♦ opening for Responder to show a positive response in hearts.

After a 2♠ heart positive, Opener has many options. The best option is that he might be able to raise hearts by bidding 3♥; that would be nice. The raise incidentally right-sides the heart contract, a bonus. He might also conceivably raise hearts with a splinter bid, with Responder's 4♦ call being a transfer back to hearts if it is available.

With no present heart support, Opener could bid Three Spades to show six or more spades.

Or, Opener could introduce a minor naturally to show four spades and five or more of the minor. Note that this meaning parallels our usual course of canapé minor rebids.

With a balanced minimum (whatever the minimum balanced range will be after you read the rest that follows), Opener can bid 3NT. We will limit this call to showing precisely 4-2-3-4 or 4-2-4-3 pattern, or possibly 4-2-5-2 or 4-2-2-5 pattern if that seems best, because of the specialized meaning of Opener's 2NT rebid. This 3NT call always denies heart support. So far, all of this is very natural stuff, within the confines of our general approach.

The one strange option for Opener is a waiting 2NT call, necessary because Responder's call has just preempted us a bit. This will typically show one of three types of hands. Opener might have a balanced minimum with specifically 5-2-3-3 pattern, which seems normal. However, Opener might also have to bid 2NT with two problem hands. Opener might have five spades and a minor that is of equal or greater length, or he might have specifically 4-1-4-4 pattern.

75

After this waiting 2NT call, Responder has the option of bidding out his hand pattern naturally. However, because 3♣ will be used as an asking bid, Responder must bid 3NT, or 4♣ if too strong to risk a pass of 3NT, to show a club-heart two-suiter.

If Responder would prefer not to describe his own hand but rather to ask for clarification of Opener's hand type, Responder can bid 3♣. This is completely artificial and asking.

After 3♣, Opener bids 3NT if he has the 5-2-3-3 balanced hand. That part is easy and logical. If Opener does rebid 3NT, Responder is expected to pass or raise the notrump call, as appropriate, or to support spades. Thus, any call except some level of spades or some level or notrumps is some sort of cuebid in support of spades.

With the 4-1-4-4 hand, Opener bids 3♦, which allows Responder to agree either minor and to show slam interest by bidding flags, meaning that 3♥ sets clubs as trumps and 3♠ sets diamond as trumps, with cuebidding following. Responder's first call had denied four spades, so the possibility of a spade fit has been ruled out.

If Opener has the spade-minor two-suited hand (five or more spades and a four-card or longer minor), he uses the same technique and "flags" his own minor. Thus, 3♥ by Opener would show a hand with at least five spades and four clubs, whereas 3♠ would show a hand with at least five spades and four diamonds. After Opener shows his minor, he may later rebid his minor to show 5-5 shape, if he wants, or he might rebid his spades with six spades, if he wants.

Responder may wish to raise one of Opener's suits after Opener shows a spade-minor two suiter by flagging his minor. Over Opener's 3♥ call (clubs and spades), everything is natural. Over Opener's 3♠ call, however, showing spades and diamonds, Responder needs an artificial call to show extra stuff with spade support, as a 4♠ raise is passable. I would suggest that the other minor call, 4♣, is a general strength raise of spades.

Opener could immediately leap over Responder's 2♠ response to four of his minor to show the big spade-minor canapé, as well.

Consider a hand from the 2008 European Bridge Team Championship. Opener holds a very strong ♠ A J 7 6 ♥ A K Q 10 7 ♦ Q J ♣ A 9. This 21-count is difficult to evaluate because of that Q-J tight in diamonds. As rebids are usually a problem for normal method 2♣ openers, some in Pau, France, reasonably opted a 1♥ opening. For us, however, the rebid problem is not as much of a concern. So, a 2♦ opening has merit. If Responder agrees spades, we are well-placed. If not, Opener can complete his nine-card pattern by rebidding 3♥, a canapé rebid showing longer hearts.

Responder, with ♠ 3 ♥ 4 2 ♦ A K 10 7 5 3 2 ♣ Q J 6, accomplishes two goals, however. First, he erases Opener's hopes of a spade fit. Second, he shows his positive response in diamonds. He responds 3♦.

Opener will find this very interesting. He will probably complete his pattern, nonetheless, with a 3♥ call, at least for now.

Responder does not like hearts either and, accordingly, could bid 3NT. He might also bid 3♠ as a punt bid because of his doubleton heart. However, a 10-count and seven diamonds to the A-K both suggest more aggressive and more focused bidding. 4♦ is my call.

Opener could not possibly stand this development, with Q-J tight in support. 7♦ must have play with this heart suit trick source. Perhaps a 4♠ call (the out-of-focus major would be RKCB for diamonds for me) makes sense. Opener can bid 4♠ as RKCB for diamonds because Opener would have jumped to 4♥ immediately over 3♦ with five spades and six hearts. If Opener were in doubt about this 4♠ call, or doubted partner's ability to field this, a straight 7♦ is certainly meritorious.

That ends the discussion of the Two Diamond opening, except for the responses and rebids after 2♦ - P - 2♥ - P - 2NT, which will be discussed with the other balanced-hand bidding in a later section, and interference concerns, which are handled in a separate section. Now we are ready to discuss the effect of this Two Diamonds opening on the Two Club opening.

SUMMARY TABLE FOR TWO DIAMOND OPENINGS

Opening Bid Requirements:

Shape:　　　　All hands with 4+ spades are opened 2♦,
　　　　　　　except 24+ balanced hands
　　　　　　　Could easily be any 4441 with spades
　　　　　　　Could easily have a longer second suit
　　　　　　　If Balanced, 22-23 HCP with 4-5 spades
Strength:　　　Strong (usually 21 HCP, but occasionally
　　　　　　　light)

Responses:

2♥	shows hands with fewer than four spades, artificial
2♠	positive with hearts (artificial), 0-3 spades
3♣	positive with clubs, 0-3 spades
3♦	positive with diamonds, 0-3 spades
3♠	positive with 5-5 in minors, 0-1 spades
2NT	positive with 4+ spade fit
3♥	weak hand with 4+ spade fit
3NT	weak diamond or heart splinter (4♣ asks which)
4♦	moderate diamond splinter
4♥	moderate heart splinter
4♣	weak or moderate club splinter (4♦ asks which)

SUMMARY, CONTINUED

<u>Opener's Rebids after 2♥ Response (not four spades, artificial relay):</u>

2♠ 5+ spades, unbalanced

2NT 4-5 spades, balanced

3♣ 4♠/5+♣, but could be 4-4-1-4
    (3♦ by Responder asks about hearts)
3♦ 4♠/5+♦, not four hearts
3♥ 4♠/5+♥

3♠ Two options:
    1. GF, sets spades as trumps,
        demands cuebidding, or
    2. Both minors and 4-1-4-4, 4-0-5-4,
        or 4-0-4-5

3NT 4♠, 4♥, 4-5♦, stiff or void in clubs,
    passable
4♣ 4♠, 4♥, 4-5♦, stiff or void in clubs, very
    strong

4♦ 5♠, 6♦, about a two-loser hand
4♥ 5♠, 6♥, about a two-loser hand
4♠ 5♠, 6♣, about a two-loser hand

SUMMARY, CONTINUED

<u>Opener's Rebids after 2♠ Artificial Response for Heart Positive:</u>

2NT   Artificial, shows one of three hand types:
1.   Precisely 5-2-3-3
2.   4-1-4-4 THREE-SUITER
3.   Five+ spades and a minor

3♣   Four spades and longer clubs (5+)
3♦   Four spades and longer diamonds (5+)

3♥   Fit for hearts
3♠   6+ spades

3NT   Precisely 4♠/2♥ and balanced

<u>Opener's Rebids after 2NT Fit-Showing Bid (Spades Agreed):</u>

3♣   Artificial relay to start cuebidding

3♦   Natural, slam probe
3♥   Natural, slam probe
3♠   Club suit, slam probe, 2-3 top spade honors
3NT   Club suit, slam probe, 0-1 top spade honors
4♣   Minimum club splinter
    (4♥ transfers to 4♠)
4♦   Minimum diamond splinter
    (4♥ transfers to 4♠)
4♠   Minimum heart splinter

THE TWO CLUBS OPENING

The second major systemic change is a result of the impact of removing almost all strong hands with four or more spades to the Two Diamonds opening. This leaves a Two Clubs strong, forcing opening that usually features at most three spades. The sole exception is when Opener has a super-strong balanced hand, meaning a hand with about 24+ HCP's and balanced. With a balanced hand of that strength, you still will open Two Clubs even with four or five spades.

Nonetheless, the removal of almost all spade-anchored hands from the Two Clubs opening has an equally amazing effect on the auctions that start with 2♣. Opener will gain an ability to show interesting patterns by using an artificial 2♠ rebid, and an artificial 3♠ rebid, for example, depending upon Responder's first call.

The best way to see the benefits, I suppose, is to describe the sequences. However, as a summary, you will learn that Opener's options after the most common of responses, a 2♦ waiting and game-forcing response, will include a 2♥ rebid, which is a Kokish Relay, showing either a super-strong balanced hand or an unbalanced hand with five or more hearts. This will be very familiar to many people.

Opener also will be able to bid 2NT, as always, showing a balanced hand. However, because Opener will not have four or five spades for this sequence, the response structure will be greatly enhanced.

Opener also will have a new tool available, a 2♠ rebid showing a heart-minor canapé hand. That means a hand with four hearts and a longer minor. This 2♠ call will also handle the specific 1-4-4-4 pattern.

Because of this new tool, Opener's minor rebids will deny four hearts. Because Opener did not open 2♦, these calls will also deny four spades. This will help tremendously in finding the correct strain.

You will also learn of a new tool, a 3♠ rebid, for Opener to use to show a 5-5 minor two-suiter, a hand pattern that is typically impossible to bid out below 3NT.

There is much more that follows, including a solution for the vexing problem of when Opener has hearts after a 2♥ double negative by Responder (simply, we will bid 2♠) and an enhanced structure for Responder to show positive responses with one or two suits.

All of this, and more, follows.

The Opening Bid of Two Clubs

Shape Requirements:

If Balanced:
  22-23 HCP, with only 2-3 spades, or
  25+ HCP, any balanced shape

If Unbalanced (Key Hand Types):
  5+ of any suit except spades, with fewer than four spades
  5-5 in the minors
  Four hearts and a longer minor, with fewer than four spades
  Specifically 1-4-4-4 shape (short spade)

Strength Requirements if Unbalanced:

  Normally, 21+ HCP
  Frequently lighter with good playing strength

When Responder has a Bust Hand

I have based the structure after the Two Clubs opening roughly on an existing and probably well-recognized style where a 2♦ response is a game-forcing waiting bid and where 2♥ is an artificial call showing a double negative. Whereas the "negative" 2♥ response to a 2♦ opening was negative only as to the spade suit and silent as to overall strength, the negative 2♥ response to a 2♣ opening is negative as to overall strength and says nothing about hearts, because a 2♣ opening does not promise four hearts. The 2♣ opening covers more territory.

The benefit to this approach is that auctions starting with a 2♦ call are enhanced by the auction being game-forcing. The major downside is when Responder bids 2♥ to show the double-negative and Opener has hearts. What is Opener to do? If he shows his suit by bidding 3♥, surely Responder must bid again. This will, however, make a 2♣ opening a game-force if Opener has hearts, because, whenever Responder has a bust hand, the auction will nonetheless be forced to game. This is quite unfortunate, and it is a cause for justifiable angst.

The 2♠ Rebid for Hearts

This problem is very quickly solved in this new approach. Had Opener held four or more spades, he would have opened 2♦, unless he has a monster balanced hand. So, after a 2♥ double negative response, Opener has no need to bid 2♠ to show spades, a suit he cannot have without being balanced and very strong.

The solution is obvious; 2♠ now is artificial and shows an unbalanced hand with at least five hearts.

The simplicity of this solution is powerful. Instead of a hand with hearts being the worst-case scenario, where Opener must rebid at the three-level after the double negative, instead Opener's cheapest available call, below 2NT at that, shows the heart hand. We will actually be pleased that we have long hearts in this auction.

After Opener's 2♠ call showing hearts, you will bid just as you would in the standard auction where partner bids 2♠ in this sequence to show spades. Nothing changes, except that you are now bidding after a call that actually showed hearts. You may think that there is one huge exception, in that Responder is preempted from bidding his spades, a suit that he could have introduced if Opener had bid 2♥ to show hearts.

But, that concern is a mirage, because the normal auction would have had Opener bidding 3♥ to show his hearts, and your spade bid would have to be at the three-level anyway. We will actually be able to bid a waiting 2NT with some spade-oriented hands, if 2NT seems best.

One note to not miss. This seems obvious, but remember that Responder just bid 2♥. There is no need to worry about re-transfers and the like. If hearts will be trumps, Responder is playing this thing. That is, unless your opponents are easily bamboozled.

Consider a problem faced at the 2008 European Bridge Team Championships in Pau, France. In the match between Denmark and Poland, for example, one team languished in a heart partscore, while the other actually played a club slam for a one-trick set, the result of an obviously difficult hand to bid! The deal follows:

♠ 8 5 4 3 2
♥ 5 3
♦ 9 8 7
♣ 6 3 2

♠ A 9 6   ♠ K Q J 7
♥ J   ♥ Q 9 4 2
♦ Q J 6 5 3 2   ♦ K 10 4
♣ 9 8 7   ♣ 10 5

♠ 10
♥ A K 10 8 7 6
♦ A
♣ A K Q J 4

In our auction, South opens 2♣ in first seat, denying four or more spades unless 24+ and balanced. North responds with a double negative 2♥, denying any Ace or King or as much as two Queens. So far, this might be a repeated sequence at many tables, albeit without the inference from our opening bid.

South now has a problem. At one table, South bid an obvious 3♥ but languished there because North, with that collection of junk, made what he thought to be a well-reasoned and practical pass.

Notice, however, how easily bid this is for us. South, having denied four spades unless he has a strong, balanced hand, can now, per our agreements, bid 2♠ to show hearts, forcing. This gives North the room to make whatever call you would prefer for this situation, whether a second-negative 2NT, the alternative of a second-negative 3♣, or a waiting 2NT, as the partnership elects. After 2NT, my choice, Opener could bid his clubs, with a jump to 4♣ if necessary to establish a forcing sequence, and the right level and strain should be reached without much pain.

This shows how that simple tweak of 2♠ to show hearts keeps the auction open, low, and manageable, with practical options restored for a bust Responder.

Other Options after a Bust 2♥ Response

All other calls are fairly standard and natural, with a few exceptions. Again, spades are largely out of the picture.

So, a 3♠ rebid is used to show a minor two-suiter. I suppose that Responder might actually have cause to flag a minor by bidding 4♥ or 4♠ if he has extreme length in the one minor and a stiff in the other minor.

Also, just as with 2♦ sequences, Opener could jump to 4♣ or 4♦ to show a Super-Canapé hand pattern with five hearts and a longer minor.

However, minor calls in this sequence will no longer deny four hearts. We are somewhat back on par with the rest of the field. We will, however, have a few advantages. Responder will use 3♠ to show 5+ spades. Also, if Responder bids 3♥, Opener can bid 3♠ as a punt bid showing 3-card heart support. Thus, Responder's 3♥ call need only show 4+ in the suit.

After a Bust Two Hearts Response

Opener Bids <u>Two Spades</u> to Show Five or More Hearts

Opener Bids Either Minor Naturally

Opener Bids <u>Three Spades</u> to Show Both Minors

Opener Bids No Trump Naturally

The Positive Responses with a Suit or Suits

With standard practice, if using 2♦ as a waiting bid and game-forcing and 2♥ as a double negative, Responder can bid 2♠, 3♣, 3♦, or 3♥ to show positive responses. The necessity to jump to 3♥ to show a heart positive makes this structure harmful to heart-focused auctions, although some have solved that problem by making a 2NT call show the heart positive. A second problem, however, with this approach is that all positive responses showing a suit are calls where the weaker side grabs declarership. Opener tables the dummy, and the lead goes through him. Not good, if it can be avoided.

I have a different approach to positive responses. None of this is necessary, as the structure can be otherwise adopted without this change, but some may find this idea useful.

Length Based Positives

Two Spades Shows One or Both Minors, Positive

Three Clubs Shows a Positive Heart Response

Three Diamonds Shows a Positive Spade Response

Three of a Major Shows a Long Suit, Weak Hand

The Positive Major Flags

With a positive response and a major, you can use flags. Thus, 3♣ would show a positive response with hearts and 3♦ a positive response with spades. This structure does not gain all that much in and of itself other than transference of who declares. Whereas there is a slight cost of preemption for Opener when

Responder shows spades, there is a slight gain when Responder shows hearts. However, the structure enables the Two Spades positive, which will be described shortly.

With a "semi-positive" major hand, something that looks like a preempt (weak with a seven-card suit), Responder can jump to three of his major (3♥ or 3♠). These could be reversed (bidding the other major) if you want.

After either of these positive responses, bidding continues naturally.

The Positive Minor(s) Relay

With one or both minors and a positive response, Responder bids 2♠. This is a "soft" relay to 2NT, meaning that Opener can express disinterest in Responder's plans and simply bid out his own hand naturally[9]. Natural calls, however, express long suits, at least six cards in length. Remember that any unbalanced hand will never feature four or more spades.

If Opener elects to hear the rest of Responder's tale, he accepts that relay and bids 2NT. Responder can then bid 3♣ or 3♦ with a one-suited positive (either bidding the suit that he has if playing naturally as much as possible, or bidding the other minor, as with the Smolen convention, if neurotic about lead transference). With a two-suited minor hand, something like 1-2-5-5 or 2-1-5-5, although 3-0 or 0-3 in the majors is possible, Responder bids his short major. Thus, 3♥ would show a

---

[9] I would expect that 3♠ must show the 24+ HCP hand with five spades, as that is the only time when Opener would have a spade suit long enough to have a fit with Responder.

minor two-suiter that approaches or is 2-1-5-5 pattern and 3♠ shows the 1-2-5-5 or a similar hand.

I have not decided for years what 2NT should show (meaning, that is, 2♣ - P - 2NT) because it seems terrible to bid that for some reason. This approach does not require that 2NT mean anything specific, as the amazing level of complexity will put you miles ahead of the competition. However, one idea is for 2NT to show a bust hand with a long minor, something that would merit a sign-off at three of the minor if Opener has a balanced minimum but that cannot be accomplished with any reasonable techniques. Using that approach, 2NT would show a weak minor. Opener could then bid 3♣ as a pass-or-correct bid, or 3♦ demanding that Responder "flag" his minor (3♥ for clubs, 3♠ for diamonds). Opener also would have the option of bidding his own heart suit at the three-level, forcing one round. Or, Opener could just blast 3NT. Again, Opener cannot have four or more spades when he is unbalanced.

Alternatively, I suppose you could reasonably use 2NT to show a bust hand with both majors (5-5).

The Waiting Positive

With any hand that merits a game-force (at least one King or two Queens), Responder will make the familiar waiting 2♦ response if he does not have a "positive response" hand. The limitations on Opener's possible patterns and strengths will add texture to the possible auctions that follow.

Again, as a matter of summary, Opener will have several options. He can bid 2♥, which is a Kokish Relay, showing either hearts (five or more) and any shape (except not 22-23 HCP and balanced) or a super-strong balanced hand (24+ HCP).

Opener also will have a new tool of 2♠, to show a hand with exactly four hearts and either a longer minor or exactly 1-4-4-4 pattern. Opener will even be able to describe immediately after this 2♠ call whether he has a three-card spade fragment or not.

Opener will be able to rebid in a minor. Those calls will be fairly normal, except that the failure to open 2♦ or rebid 2♠ eliminates the possibility of Opener having a side four-card major. This will help to ensure that Responder needs five cards in a major to introduce them. Responder will even be able to describe 5-5 in the majors effectively and below 3NT.

Opener will also have another new tool, a 3♠ call to show the difficult minor two-suiter without bypassing 3NT.

Also, in a parallel to auctions starting with a 2♦ opening, Opener can jump to 4♣ or 4♦ as his next call to show a Super-Canapé hand, meaning five hearts and a longer minor.

As always, there is much more to the story.

Opener's Main Options After Game-Forcing Artificial Two Diamonds Response

Two Hearts as a Kokish Relay

   Five or More Hearts (Not Four Spades) or

   24+ Balanced (Could Have 2, 3, 4, or 5 Spades)

Two Spades Shows Four Hearts and...

   Longer Minor, or

   Specifically 1-4-4-4 Shape (short spades)

Two No Trump Shows 22-23 HCP With Only Two or Three Spades

Three Clubs or Three Diamonds are Natural, but No Four-Card Major

Three Spades is Artificial with Minor Two-Suiter

Kokish Two Hearts by Opener

If you know about a Kokish 2♥ rebid, then this part should be somewhat familiar, albeit with some nice tools enabled by the limitation on the spade length held by Opener.

A Kokish 2♥ rebid by Opener is designed to solve a problem of the super-strong balanced hand. Opening 2♣ and then jumping to 3NT to show a hand with 24 or more HCP seems dumb. When life is good for us, why preempt our side out of a good, constructive auction to a possible slam? Eric Kokish suggested an interesting idea that has become mainstream with many good players, namely that a 2♥ rebid by a 2♣ Opener shows either hearts or any very strong balanced hand.

Responder is expected to bid 2♠ to allow Opener to clarify his holding. With the super-strong, balanced hand, Opener bids 2NT, negating any natural meaning to the 2♥ call. Opener might have five hearts, or he might have only two of them, or any number in between. The 2NT call simply establishes that Opener has a balanced hand with 24+ HCP and that the 2♥ call was artificial to save space for the partnership.

If Opener has hearts, he bids naturally after the 2♠ relay, maybe introducing a new suit or maybe rebidding his hearts with extra length, or perhaps bidding 3NT.

I have messed around with Kokish somewhat, on one level because of a humorous story and on another because of the impact of Opener denying four spades when he is unbalanced.

Responder's Alternatives to Kokish 2♠

One change concerns giving Responder an option other than following blindly and simply bidding 2♠ like a trained seal.

A few years ago, I was playing in a local club game with three friends. Each thought he was the best player at the table. That debate remains undecided by vote but very decided if you ask any one of us. My LHO opened 2♣, his partner bid 2♦, and he bid 2♥, alerted as "Kokish." When his partner bid 2♠, my LHO neglected to alert because his partner had explained that 2♥ was a relay to 2♠. I, nonetheless, asked my LHO what 2♠ showed. My LHO looked at me like I was an idiot and then clarified that his look was honest – he actually did think that I was an idiot and made that very clear.

This, of course, made me mad. So, I decided that I had to create meanings for bids that Responder might make other than 2♠. I decided that a 4-4-4-1 hand was a difficult hand for Responder to bid if Opener happened to be balanced and that a splinter might be a useful piece of information if Opener held hearts. I also decided that a splinter into *hearts* in support of a new suit shown by Opener, with hearts and that new suit, would be impossible to bid but also possibly useful.

So, my change, inspired by my good but occasionally annoying bridge friend, is that Responder can reject the Kokish relay to 2♠ and instead bid a stiff if he has 4-4-4-1 pattern. With a stiff spade, the highest stiff that can be shown, maybe you can save space and bid 2NT instead.

After making this call, Opener should be fairly well-placed. Imagine, first, that he has a heart fit after a 2NT (1-4-4-4), 3♣ (4-4-4-1), or 3♦ call. Whether

Opener started with five hearts and an unbalanced hand or 4-5 hearts and a super-strong balanced hand, he can now bid 3♥ to set trumps, and cuebidding starts. Responder already has shown his shortness and his complete shape.

If Opener has the super-strong balanced hand, or a tactical reason for doing so, he can also set either minor as trumps over 2NT (1-4-4-4) by bidding the minor. Similarly, over 3♣ (4-4-4-1), Opener with the super-strong balanced hand can set either diamonds (3♦) or spades (3♠) as trumps. Over 3♦ (4-4-1-4), Opener might have a slight problem if he wants to set clubs as trumps, in that he must commit to bypassing 3NT if so inclined. In any event, Opener can also reject all suits by bidding 3NT, which nonetheless shows a very strong balanced hand, or even 4NT or higher if strong enough.

Over 3♥ (4-1-4-4), Opener must enter the four-level to set a minor as trumps. He might even opt to bid 4♥ to play with the right hand.

When Opener has the Super-Strong Balanced Hand

Assuming a 2♠ reply from Responder, Opener bids 2NT to show 24+ HCP. In the prior section about the 2♦ opening, I mentioned an intention to describe in a separate section the techniques used when Opener has a strong, balanced hand. I will also defer this discussion of the super-strong balanced hands for that section. Suffice it to say that, for now, Opener's 2NT bid at this point shows the super-strong hand. In that sole event, Opener might have four, or even five, spades.

When Opener Has the Unbalanced Hand with Hearts

As with normal Kokish, Opener shows the unbalanced hand with hearts by bidding a new minor, or rebidding hearts, or perhaps even 3NT. There is one improvement on this familiar sequence, however, because of the limitation on Opener's spade length. Opener will never rebid 3♠ to show five hearts and four spades. That call might be used for some interesting meaning, if you want. My personal preference is to have this call promise three spades and six hearts. Otherwise, the Kokish sequences are fairly standard.

Some Practical Analysis

A deal from the 2004 Olympiad is worth study. Dealer, you hold ♠ J ♥ A K 9 4 2 ♦ A J ♣ A K Q 8 4. What do you open? There are technically 22 HCP, but the two Jacks each look suspect. Plus, despite the strength of this hand, rebids will be a problem for standard bidders who open 2♣ and hear a 2♥ double negative response. This resulted in some people opening 1♥ and catching up. For us, this hand pattern is less troubling. If we hear the 2♥ double negative response, we can bid 2♠ to show the heart suit, which leaves us space to bid the club suit after a possible 2NT call from Responder.

In practice, however, Responder has a positive response. With no positive suit, he bids the game-forcing 2♦. Opener bids 2♥ Kokish, and Responder, who is not 4-4-4-1, bids 2♠. Opener clarifies shape and that his heart suit is real with a 3♣ rebid.

The Minor-Heart Canapé Two Spades Rebid

Let us return to the start of the auction. Opener started with a 2♣ opening, usually denying four or more spades (absolutely if Opener is unbalanced). Responder has just bid 2♦, game-forcing and "waiting."

At this common juncture, standard methods would leave Opener with a problem if he has five of a minor, four of a major, and an unbalanced hand. A sixth card in the minor helps little. Opener might solve his own problem by just bidding the minor, but that transfers the problem to Responder. The system has a flaw. If Responder is allowed to bid four-card majors, should Opener raise with three-card support? If not, will we not miss the 5-3 fit? If your solution is to require that Responder have five of his major, then will this not make it impossible to find the 4-4 major fit?

One classic solution is Giorgio Belladonna's idea to have a jump to three of a major show four of that major and long diamonds, but that is quite preemptive. It also causes obvious difficulties if Opener has, for example, 4-3-5-1 or 4-3-6-0 shape, where the best strain may be the preempted hearts. The club-based hands can be helped with a waiting 3♦ call, but that also has its own problems.

As we discussed previously, this problem evaporates for us when Opener has four spades and a longer minor and opens 2♦, showing four or more spades. Plus, we found out that we were even able to have Responder raise that minor below 3NT with our new techniques. Well, the 2♠ rebid by Opener after a 2♣ opening and a game-forcing 2♦ response is the solution for the minor-heart canapé problem.

Opener's 2♠ rebid in this sequence (2♣-P-2♦-P-2♠) is an artificial call, showing precisely four hearts and an unbalanced hand. This unbalanced hand,

98

because it cannot feature a spade suit, will necessarily be a hand with four hearts and a longer minor or precisely 1-4-4-4 pattern (or 0-4-5-4/0-4-4-5, which technically meets the first definition anyway).

If Responder has a Heart Fit

As after a 2♦ opening, where Responder immediately sets trumps when he has four-card or longer support for Opener's known four-card or longer spade suit, so also Responder immediately agrees hearts when he has four-card or longer support for Opener's now known four-card heart suit after this 2♠ rebid. The benefits are roughly the same. First, cuebidding starts earlier. Second, the failure to raise hearts allows heart calls later to be artificial, because a heart fit has been ruled out already.

So, when Responder does have four-card or longer support for hearts, he immediately cuebids with calls above 2NT, including possible jumps. Again, your stylistic choices as to how to cuebid, or whether pattern bidding is used, or spiral scans, or whatever, are largely irrelevant to the foundational method. The idea is to agree on something that you and partner like and to use that technique. Whatever you use, you will be ahead of the folks who might not even be able to find the four-four heart fit.

Also, just as after the 2♦ Opening sequences where spades are immediately agreed, you may desire to adjust your techniques to enable Opener to bid hearts first.

My suggested approach would be for Responder to usually start with a 3♣ all-purpose relay, to allow Opener to complete the picture of his hand and thereby to enable the same type of definition to his rebids as would assist with that parallel 2♦ opening and immediate spade raise.

After the normal 3♣ call, Opener would normally bid 3♦ with a longer diamond suit, 3♥ with a longer club suit, or 3♠ with 1-4-4-4 shape. Opener could also make Picture Jumps to 4♣ or 4♦, bidding the longer minor and indicating that the stiff is in the other minor. 3NT for clubs and 4♥ for diamonds would also be Picture Jumps, showing the indicated minor and that the stiff is in spades. The Picture Jump bids should show control of all suits with about a four loser hand.

Opener's Options After 3♣ Agreeing Hearts	
• Three Diamonds	Shows Four Hearts, Five or More Diamonds
• Three Hearts	Shows Four Hearts, Five or More Clubs
• Three Spades	Shows 1-4-4-4 Shape (Short Spade)
• Four Clubs	Shows Long Clubs, Picture Bid, with Short Diamonds
• Four Diamonds	Shows Long Diamonds, Picture Bid, with Short Clubs
• Three No Trump	Shows Long Clubs, Picture Bid, with Short Spades
• Four Hearts	Shows Long Diamonds, Picture Bid, with Short Spades

Thus, something like ♠ A K x ♥ A Q 10 x ♦ A K J x x ♣ x would be perfect for a 4♦ Picture Jump, and ♠ A K x ♥ A Q 10 x ♦ x ♣ A K J x x would merit a 4♣ Picture Jump. With ♠ x ♥ A Q 10 x ♦ A K J x x ♣ A K x, Opener could make a Picture

Jump to 4♥, flagging the diamond suit as the long suit and indicating shortness in spades, whereas with ♠ x ♥ A Q 10 x ♦ A K x ♣ A K J x x Opener would bid 3NT to flag the club suit and show the stiff spade.

Obviously, then, a straight 3♦ call, showing longer diamonds, or a 3♥ call, showing longer clubs, would show a different hand. Perhaps Opener has no stiff. Perhaps Opener lacks control in one of the suits. Perhaps Opener has a worse hand (unlikely) or a better hand.

Responder would also have alternatives to the generic 3♣ call. The first alternative would be a 3♦ call, showing an undisclosed stiff. If Opener wants to know the location of the stiff, which will often be the case, he bids 3♥, which incidentally also captures declarership. Responder bids 3♠ with a stiff spade, 3NT with a stiff diamond, or 4♣ with a stiff club. 4♦ would show a void in diamonds and 4♥ a void in clubs. Opener could decline to ask and just bid out his own hand, as well, with 3♠ still the 1-4-4-4 hand, but now bidding his minor naturally at the four-level.

With a spade void, Responder immediately bids 3NT over Opener's 2♠, to catch the missing holding.

Responder could also make a sort of "fit jump," bidding 3♠, 4♣, or 4♦ to show a concentration of values in the indicated suit, with no other side controls. The suit should be quality, something like KQ10x as a minimum.

Responder could bid 3♥, a bid that makes him declarer, with the rare hand of three side Kings.

Responder's Options to Generic 3♣ Agreeing Hearts

- **Three Diamonds**   Shows Undisclosed Stiff or Minor Void

   Opener's 3♥ Asks:

3♠	= Stiff Spade
3NT	= Stiff Diamond
4♣	= Stiff Club
4♦	= Void Diamonds
4♥	= Void Clubs

- **Three No Trump**   Shows Spade Void (Missing Void)

- **Three Spades**   Fit Bid (Good Spades, No Minor Controls)

- **Four Clubs**   Fit Bid (Good Clubs, No Spade or Diamond Controls)

- **Four Diamonds**   Fit Bid (Good Diamonds, No Spade or Club Controls)

- **Three Hearts**   All Three Side Kings

An example from the 2006 Rosenblum, in Verona:

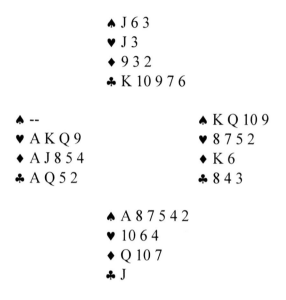

♠ J 6 3
♥ J 3
♦ 9 3 2
♣ K 10 9 7 6

♠ --
♥ A K Q 9
♦ A J 8 5 4
♣ A Q 5 2

♠ K Q 10 9
♥ 8 7 5 2
♦ K 6
♣ 8 4 3

♠ A 8 7 5 4 2
♥ 10 6 4
♦ Q 10 7
♣ J

Dealer West opens 2♣, a strong, forcing opening denying four spades (unless super-strong and balanced). East, lacking any ability to make a positive response in a suit, but having a game-forcing hand, responds with a waiting and game-forcing 2♦ call. Opener shows a heart-minor canapé, or a 1-4-4-4 hand, by bidding 2♠.

Using my recommended techniques, Responder can immediately agree hearts by bidding 3♣, a relay that tends to deny a stiff or void on the outside and tends to deny a concentration of values in one suit. Although he does have a suit of sufficient values in spades, his values are not "concentrated" because he has the diamond King, as well.

Opener can then either describe his hand as a three-suited hand by bidding 3♠ to show 1-4-4-4 shape or indicate that diamonds is his longer suit by bidding

3♦. Either way, a problem hand becomes much simpler to bid.

Even with simple cuebidding, Responder would cuebid 3♦ to show the diamond control, followed by a trump cuebid (3♥) by Opener because his hearts are so good, and a 3♠ cue by Responder. This is also a superior auction to anything most folks would experience with this difficult pair of hands.

Another problem deal is rather easy for us, a deal from the 2008 European Bridge Team Championship. Belarus and Poland each reached 6♥ with this collection, missing the very solid grand slam. I think we do better, with a simple auction.

♠ Q 5
♥ A K Q 6
♦ A K Q 10 5 3
♣ 3

♠ K 7	♠ J 10 8 6 2
♥ 8 3	♥ 9 7 4
♦ J 4 2	♦ 9
♣ K J 8 7 6 2	♣ Q 10 9 4

♠ A 9 4 3
♥ J 10 5 2
♦ 8 7 6
♣ A 5

After three passes, North, recognizing the playing strength of his hand, opens a reasoned 2♣. South makes a positive 2♦ waiting response. North now bids 2♠ to show an unbalanced hand with four hearts, whether 1-4-4-4 or a heart-minor canapé hand.

South has a heart fit, so he shows that immediately with a non-committal 3♣, again tending to deny shortness or a concentration of values. North continues with 3♦, showing that his diamonds are longer than his hearts. Responder bypasses 3♥, whether because you opt to have Opener bid hearts first or because you make unfettered cues and South lacks any reason to cue trumps. Either way, Responder next cues his spade control by bidding 3♠.

When North grabs the carrot and launches into RKCB, he later has enough information to know that the decision turns on whether hearts splitting 3-2 is sufficiently reliable to bid the grand. Whether he opts the grand or the safe small slam, the auction is nonetheless very simple.

You may notice, however, that this hand pattern looks fairly easy to handle with Opener starting 1♦ and then leaping to 4♦ after Responder bids 1♥. That also would be a fair way to bid this hand, especially if the spade suit was a tad weaker. If the spade suit had been ♠ K x, a 2♣ opening stands out. That ♠ Q x is hard to value.

I would much rather, however, that I have two *good* options than that I have no idea how to handle this holding with either start.

Another deal, from the 2008 Cavendish Teams, is interesting.

```
                  ♠ 6 5 4
                  ♥ 10 5 2
                  ♦ 10 9 6
                  ♣ A 10 9 3

♠ Q 7 2                        ♠ A K 10
♥ 9 8 7 4 3                    ♥ A Q J 6
♦ 3                            ♦ A K J 5 2
♣ Q J 6 4                      ♣ 2

                  ♠ J 9 8 3
                  ♥ K
                  ♦ Q 8 7 4
                  ♣ K 8 7 5
```

West deals and passes, as does North. East has one of those difficult hands for most people, but this is no problem for us. He opens 2♣ and hears a waiting 2♦ response, game forcing, from West. East then announces four hearts with either a longer minor or 1-4-4-4 pattern by rebidding the artificial 2♠. He will bid 3♠ to show a fragment (three cards) in spades and longer diamonds if Responder bids 2NT.

Instead, Responder has heart support and can show that immediately. With a stiff in diamonds, Responder first bids 3♦, showing undisclosed shortness. Opener relays 3♥ to ask where it is, and West bids 3NT to show that his stiff is in diamonds. Had he held a void in diamonds, he would have bid 4♦.

The 3NT bid showing a diamond splinter does not interest East as much as West hoped. On a conservative day, East will sign off and avoid the failing slam (single dummy) that one team suffered. I might bid on anyway and suffer that same poor result, unfortunately, unless I wised up and declined to bid a slam on a hook.

If Responder Has No Fit for Hearts

When Responder lacks four hearts, he accepts an implied "relay" and bids 2NT, allowing Opener to clarify his pattern.

You might think of this structure as the second of two "Kokish" relays. Whereas Opener's 2♥ rebid is a relay to 2♠ so that Opener can show an unbalanced hand with *five* hearts, Opener's 2♠ rebid is a relay to 2NT so that Opener can show an unbalanced hand with *four* hearts and a longer second suit. Whereas Opener's 2♥ relay might also be based upon a very strong balanced hand as the single exception, the 2♠ relay might be based on the specific pattern of 1-4-4-4 as the single exception to the usual expectation that there is a second suit longer than hearts. Finally, whereas Responder can reject the 2♥ Kokish relay with any hand with a stiff and three four-card suits, Responder will reject the 2♠ relay whenever he has support for hearts.

In any event, when Responder lacks four hearts, he bids 2NT as the relay to allow Opener to complete the pattern of his hand.

Opener's Options After Responder's 2NT

Three No Trump

>   Shows 1-4-4-4 pattern

Four Clubs

>   Same 1-4-4-4 pattern, but REALLY STRONG

Three Clubs or *Three Diamonds*

>   Four Hearts, Longer Minor, Not Three Spades

Three Hearts

>   Four Hearts, Longer Clubs, Three Spades

Three Spades

>   Four Hearts, Longer Diamonds, Three Spades

With the 1-4-4-4 hands

Opener can bid 3NT to show the 1-4-4-4 pattern, or 4♣ to show the same pattern with too strong a hand to allow Responder to possibly pass 3NT. Bidding is somewhat natural thereafter, except that Responder might need to bid 4♠ after 4♣ to agree clubs.[10] Opener is allowed to show a hand with 0-4-4-5 or 0-4-5-4 pattern as if he were 1-4-4-4, if that makes sense to him as the best description of his hand.[11]

With Four Hearts and a Longer Minor

Opener more often has a heart-minor canapé, meaning exactly four hearts and a longer minor. With that holding, Opener can provide quite amazing definition to his hand pattern.

The primary task is to identify the long minor. However, Opener has enough room to also indicate whether he does or does not have three spades, which will help if Responder has a five-card spade suit that he

---

[10] Over this call, some may like using the cheapest call as an artificial relay showing no interest in anything exciting. Thus, after 3NT, Responder could bid 4♣ as a relay to 4♦ in preparation for a sign-off suggestion of 4♥, 5♣, or 5♦. With better values, Responder immediately bids 4♦, 4♥, or 5♣ (natural if so desired, or as transfers to the next suit up, the suit of preference, if even more science is desired). Similarly, after 4♣ from Opener (same hand pattern but stronger), 4♦ would be the relay (Responder might pass 4♥) or Responder would bid the suit of interest if slammish.

[11] Alternatively, I suppose you could treat a 4♦ call as a 0-4-5-4 hand and 4♥ as 0-4-4-5.

has not been able to bid. When Responder bids his minor over 2NT, whether 3♣ or 3♦, these calls show the minor bid but also deny three spades.

When Opener does have a three-card spade suit, Opener "flags" his minor, meaning 3♥ for clubs and 3♠ for diamonds.

The Heart-Minor Canapé with a Spade Fragment

Explaining this flagging concept in more detail might be a good idea. If Opener has 3-4-1-5 or 3-4-0-6 pattern (a club-heart canapé with three spades), he "flags" the club suit by bidding 3♥. With 3-4-5-1 or 3-4-6-0 pattern (a diamond-heart canapé with three spades), Opener "flags" his diamond suit by bidding 3♠. Thus, the major calls (3♥ and 3♠) both show a spade fragment and identify the minor by rank. This more complete pattern description might enable better consideration of 3NT as a final contract, might enable finding a 5-3 spade fit more quickly, and might provide useful information for a possible slam in the minor.

After the spade-fragment minor-heart canapé calls (3♥ or 3♠), Responder can reciprocate the flagging technique as well. If Responder wants to suggest bigger and better things in Opener's minor, Responder bids the minor at the four-level. If Responder wants to agree spades and show extra strength, Responder either bids 3♠ if available (after a 3♥ rebid by Opener) or bids 4♣, the other minor, if 3♠ is not available (after Opener's 3♠ rebid). With a minimum, Responder can use fast arrival and jump to 4♠ or even five of Opener's minor.

Transfers are not a concern because Opener opened 2♣, Responder then bid 2♦, and Opener rebid 2♠. We already know who will declare the final contract.

The Heart-Minor Canapé without a Spade Fragment

Again, if Opener has a minor-heart canapé (four hearts, longer in the minor) but does not have three spades, he just bids his minor (3♣ or 3♦). These calls deny three spades and thus typically show six or more of the long minor, or a fragment in the other minor, or 2-4-2-5/2-4-5-2 pattern. 0-4-4-5 or 0-4-5-4 is also possible.

After a natural minor call, Responder has a great option that is not obvious, enabled because the heart suit has been eliminated as a possible strain. He could, of course, bid 3♠ naturally, showing a six-card or longer spade suit that was not good enough for a positive response. If Opener bids 3♣, Responder could also bid 3♦ naturally, as well. The neat new tool, however, is that Responder can raise the minor below 3NT by bidding 3♥. Hearts has been eliminated as a possible strain, freeing the heart call as a raise of Opener's long minor.

Responder could also make a very strong raise of the minor by bidding four of the minor. Thus, the raise of the minor by way of an artificial 3♥ call is treated in the same manner as the artificial raise of Opener's minor by way of an artificial 3♠ bid in the parallel auction where Opener shows spades instead of hearts by Opening 2♦. The 3♥ option in this sequence shows either an inclination to have Opener consider 3NT, or a lesser contribution to the minor fit, or general uncertainty, whereas the four-level raise is the power raise.

If Opener hears 3♥ and bids 3NT, this is an offer to play. Opener can also bid 3♠ artificially, suggesting disinterest in 3NT, either because of stopper problems or because Opener has a very strong hand and slam interest.

Note how nice it is for Opener to be able to show a minor that is only five cards long this way. Most folks would expect six cards if Opener introduces a minor at the three-level after opening 2♣, and that the hand is extremely strong. For us, Opener might have a five-card suit and a relatively mediocre strong, forcing opening. No problems.

An example from Shanghai illustrates the power of this treatment. East sat in third seat and held ♠ -- ♥ A K Q 5 ♦ A 6 5 4 3 ♣ A Q J 7. A 20-point hand with great playing strength. Most people would and did open this hand 1♦. That may be the best course even if using our techniques. However, as an illustrative hand, consider the option of opening 2♣. Using standard techniques, a 2♣ opening seems horrible. After any expected response, there is a rebid problem. The idea of bidding 3♦ on that meager of a suit is not appealing. Thus, even with a bit more in the way of HCP strength, 2♣ is not appealing for standard 2♣ openers.

How about when you open 2♣ our way? Well, let us play out the actual auction with the actual deal to see:

♠ Q J 7 5 4
♥ 4
♦ J 10 7 2
♣ K 8 5

♠ A K 3   ♠ --
♥ 10 8 7 6   ♥ A K Q 5
♦ 9   ♦ A 6 5 4 3
♣ 10 9 6 3 2   ♣ A Q J 7

♠ 10 9 8 6 2
♥ J 9 3 2
♦ K Q 8
♣ 4

Responder has no positive with a suit, but he does have enough for a game-forcing 2♦ response. This allows Opener to bid 2♠ with intent to show a heart-minor canapé, four hearts and a longer minor. Opener might be debating whether describing 1-4-4-4 shape would be a better description of this hand, or even whether he has enough to show specifically 0-4-5-4 shape with that 4♦ second rebid option in the footnote. Who else has three different reasonable options with this hand?

As Responder has a heart fit, though, he does not bid 2NT as a relay, instead bidding whatever you have agreed as a heart raise. Maybe a 4♦ splinter? How nice would that option be rewarded, if Opener is careful to bid 6♣ as a choice-of-slams bid eventually?

Using my suggested continuations, Responder would bid 3♦ to show an undisclosed splinter, and Opener could bid 3♥ to confirm the whereabouts of the stiff. Sure enough, West has shortness in diamonds, and it is a stiff, so he bids 3NT. Had Responder held a void

113

in diamonds, he would bid 4♦. But, over 3NT, Opener could cue 4♣, allowing Responder to cue 4♠ before Opener makes his move, eventually offering clubs as an alternative contract.

Had Responder held only three hearts, a 2NT relay would have allowed Opener to show his diamond suit. We would still be at 3♦ without a fit, but at least Opener's hand would have been much better described, and a heart fit ruled out. That would allow Responder to bid 3♥, when appropriate, to agree diamonds below 3NT, a technique that no one else will have available.

Consider also this deal, from the 2008 European Bridge Team Championship:

```
              ♠ K Q 4
              ♥ J 7 6 5
              ♦ A 7 3 2
              ♣ 10 3

♠ J 9 6 5 2              ♠ A
♥ Q 8                    ♥ A K 4 3
♦ Q 6                    ♦ K J 9
♣ Q J 7 5                ♣ A K 9 6 4

              ♠ 10 8 7 3
              ♥ 10 9 2
              ♦ 10 8 5 4
              ♣ 8 2
```

East is Dealer. This is a classic problem for standard bidding. With 22 HCP, a 2♣ opening comes to mind. However, with four losers and a meager club suit, the idea of opening 2♣ to rebid 3♣ is offensive. Most would opt for the more practical 1♣ opening and hope to catch up.

Again, however, this rebid problem is for us not a problem but an asset. East opens 2♣, and West responds with a positive, waiting 2♦. East now bids 2♠, artificially showing four hearts and either a longer minor or specifically 1-4-4-4 shape.

West lacks a heart fit. Had he held four hearts, the heart fit would immediately be found. However, this time he must rebid 2NT as a relay to find out what Opener had.

Opener, with a club-heart canapé hand, completes his pattern while simultaneously describing his spade length. Had Opener held 3-4-1-5 pattern, which would have greatly interested West with his five spades, Opener would have rebid 3♥, a flag for the lower minor, clubs, promising a spade fragment (three cards). Lacking that, Opener simply rebids his minor naturally, 3♣. Remember that 3NT would have shown 1-4-4-4 pattern and that 4♣ would have shown that 1-4-4-4 pattern with massive values.

Anyway, after 3♣, West knows that a spade fit has been ruled out. With a nice collection of possibly well-placed Queens, however, and a really fine club fit, West is both concerned about a 3NT game and also interested in a possible slam. Two clear cover cards and a third possible cover card, plus that doubleton heart with four trumps, all looks rather promising. So, what does Responder bid?

Responder has a nice call of 3♥. Remember, when hearts has been ruled out as a possible strain, a 3♥ call serves as a raise of Opener's minor below 3NT. Perfect! Because Opener was able to deny three spades, Responder was able to disregard the spade fit and focus on the one remaining important asset in his hand – the club fit.

East now has a tough decision. With this unbalanced hand, and a raise of his clubs, he must decide whether to try for the unknown 3NT or embark on a club slam adventure, with 5♣ as the alternative if the slam is not there. If Opener makes the right decision for this hand, he could blast out a 4♠ call, if that would be read as a splinter in your techniques. Alternatively, he could complete his pattern with a 4♦ call if that would be your preferred style. He might even make a simple non-descript waiting/probe bid of 3♠.

In any event, West eventually will know that even his diamond Queen is working and can make noise.

How about a 1-4-4-4 hand, from Pau:

            ♠ A 10 8 7
            ♥ K 7 5
            ♦ 10 8 2
            ♣ J 5 2

♠ K J 9 3   ♠ 6 5 4 2
♥ ---   ♥ Q J 10 8 6 3
♦ 7 6 3   ♦ J 9 5
♣ Q 10 9 8 7 6   ♣ ---

            ♠ Q
            ♥ A 9 4 2
            ♦ A K Q 4
            ♣ A K 4 3

South is looking at 22 HCP, but many would opt for a 1♦ opening because of the anticipated rebid problems caused by the 1-4-4-4 pattern after a normal 2♣ opening. We, however, have no real problems with that pattern. Accordingly, South opens 2♣.

116

Assuming no intervention (as occurred in at least one match), North responds with the obvious 2♦ GF relay, and South completes the first part of his picture by rebidding 2♠, showing four hearts and either a longer minor or specifically 1-4-4-4 shape.

Had North held a fourth heart, North would support hearts immediately, with a 3♣ relay if using my proposed methods. This time, however, North bids 2NT as a relay to hear what Opener has.

Opener has 1-4-4-4 pattern and must, therefore, pick between 3NT and 4♣, the latter showing a powerhouse 1-4-4-4 hand too good to risk Responder passing 3NT. South, however, has no problem making his choice. 3NT is his call.

North is thankful for his spade 10 and will be very thankful for that stiff Queen. In any event, the pass is obvious. An easy sequence, again.

One more quick deal, from the 2008 World Mind Sports Games in Beijing.

Opener: ♠ A ♥ J 9 4 3 ♦ A K Q 8 4 ♣ K Q 9
Responder: ♠ 7 5 2 ♥ Q ♦ J 10 9 ♣ A 6 5 4 3 2

Opener starts with a 2♣ opening (not four spades).

Responder might consider a 2♠ response, planning to show a positive response with clubs. This would actually work well, as Opener (who would be shocked by how good his clubs are) would clearly relay 2NT and then move hard at a club slam, especially after finding out about the heart control. However, our Responder wants better clubs for a positive and opts for a 2♦ waiting bid, game-forcing. A reasonable alternative.

Opener now bids 2♠, showing four hearts and either a longer minor or specifically 1-4-4-4 shape.

Responder could have set trumps immediately with heart support. However, lacking that, Responder bids 2NT, a relay asking Opener to explain his shape.

Opener has two options with four hearts and longer diamonds. He either bids 3♦ naturally, which also denies three spades, or he "flags" diamonds by bidding 3♠, showing longer diamonds with three spades (3♥ would have flagged clubs and shown longer clubs with three spades). Our Opener bids 3♦ because he lacks three spades.

This looks interesting to Responder. He smells a likely stiff from Opener in spades, which cannot be bad. He is not sure whether the heart stiff, the heart Queen, or both are important, but the stiff Queen must be interesting somehow. The diamond sequence is nice. Furthermore, the long club suit seems reasonably likely to be opposite some support, although a stiff works fine. In any event, Responder has an easy call – 3♥. Remember that when hearts is eliminated as a strain, that suit operates as a surrogate for raising the minor. Here, Responder can "raise" diamonds below 3NT by bidding 3♥, a suit that cannot be trumps. Alternatively, a straight splinter of 4♥ might even be considered by Responder.

Straight Minor Rebids

After 2♣-P-2♦, Opener might also rebid 3♣ or 3♦, which are both natural calls as is played normally. However, for us, each of these bids denies a four-card major, because Opener would have bid 2♣ and then 2♠ with four hearts, or would have opened 2♦ with four spades. This takes some stress off, because Responder can now bid the majors confident that showing a five-card suit costs nothing.

A deal from the 2005 Bermuda Bowl in Estoril illustrates an unexpected gain from knowing that Opener lacks any four-card major when he opens 2♣ and then rebids a minor.

The deal:

```
                    ♠ A K 2
                    ♥ 8
                    ♦ A K Q 10 6 2
                    ♣ A 9 5

  ♠ 9 6 4 3                         ♠ J 10 8 7
  ♥ Q 7 6 5 2                       ♥ A 9
  ♦ 8                               ♦ J 9 4
  ♣ K 6 3                           ♣ 10 8 7 2

                    ♠ Q 5
                    ♥ K J 10 4 3
                    ♦ 7 5 3
                    ♣ Q J 4
```

North opens 2♣ in second seat. Sure, this is a mere 20-count, but the primed hand and nearly solid suit merits a 2♣ opening. South has almost enough for a positive response in hearts, but not quite. So, he bids a simple 2♦. There is plenty of space with which to introduce hearts later. Opener completes his general picture of a diamond one-suiter with no four-card major by rebidding 3♦.

South now bids his hearts, 3♥. This shows a five-card suit because Opener has denied four hearts. Back to North. Now, think this hand through from the perspective of a possible problem for South. What if South had held 5-5 in the majors, something like ♠Q x x x x ♥ K J 10 x x ♦ x ♣ x x? Does South force the four-level when there may be no major fit at all? No problem for us. South bids his hearts, comfortable that North, who has denied four spades, can bid 3♠ when he has a three-card spade suit. In practice, North's 3♠ rebid does not interest South, who resigns to 3NT.

Notice the inversion from normal thinking. One would normally expect South to bid spades and then hearts if holding 5-5 in the majors. However, North's ability to bid a three-card spade fragment frees South to bid the majors up the line and thereby to stay below 3NT while exploring the majors.

Now, you may think to yourself at this point that perhaps this wrong-sides 3NT contracts too much. This is a fair concern. If this troubles you, then you could agree that Opener bids 3NT in this sequence when he has three spades and bids 3♠ when he lacks three spades. That switcheroo makes some sense, as Opener is more likely to have three spades when he lacks heart support and may be concerned about playing 3NT with those hands where he does lack three spades.

Another Estoril deal provides the same benefit analysis:

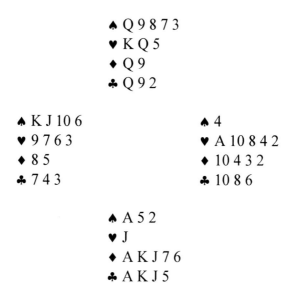

♠ Q 9 8 7 3
♥ K Q 5
♦ Q 9
♣ Q 9 2

♠ K J 10 6   ♠ 4
♥ 9 7 6 3   ♥ A 10 8 4 2
♦ 8 5   ♦ 10 4 3 2
♣ 7 4 3   ♣ 10 8 6

♠ A 5 2
♥ J
♦ A K J 7 6
♣ A K J 5

Now, sitting third seat with the South hand, no one using standard methods would even dream of opening 2♣. In practice, a 1♦ opening was selected by USA II, a typical and practical start. However, the end result was that the spade fit was lost. The auction was:

1♦	P	1♠	P
3♣	P	3NT	P
P	P		

That is probably the best sequence and contract anyway.

However, imagine if one were to move the heart Jack to spades, which makes this a reasonable 21-count. Just to see how powerful the technique is, let us open that South hand 2♣. After North shows a positive hand without a positive suit by bidding the game-forcing 2♦,

South introduces his diamonds and denies a four-card major by bidding 3♦. This allows North to show *five* spades when he bids 3♠, and the spade fit is located.

Thus, whereas with standard methods a minor-based hand pattern is a problem that merits a practical one-level opening, for us the 2♣ opening coupled with the inferences from not opening 2♦, and the inferences on a minor rebid from not rebidding 2♠ to show a heart-minor canapé, combine to give us the ability to decide between different options with more flexibility. We are not cornered into our opening bid as often.

Now, admittedly I would not open this hand 2♣ even with all of this, because a 3♦ rebid still sounds a lot like a six-card suit. But, move one of the clubs over to the diamonds and you get my point.

Consider, as well, a more appropriate deal from the European Bridge Team Championships in 2008. Some missed the spade fit, which seems understandable. The deal:

```
                    ♠ J 8
                    ♥ J 7 6 5 4
                    ♦ 9 6 4
                    ♣ 8 4 2

    ♠ A Q 7                        ♠ 10 5 4 3 2
    ♥ A Q                          ♥ 10 9 8
    ♦ K 10                         ♦ A 5 3
    ♣ A Q J 9 7 3                  ♣ K 6

                    ♠ K 9 6
                    ♥ K 3 2
                    ♦ Q J 8 7 2
                    ♣ 10 5
```

After a pass from South, West first must decide what to open. With 22 HCP's, a 2♣ opening comes to mind. However, because of the inadequate agreements after the obvious 3♣ rebid, that rebid usually shows a huge hand, with about four losers as the worst holding, and this hand has a solid four losers, perhaps slightly worse. Treating this as a balanced hand has some appeal, but evaluating this fit-dependent hand properly is difficult. When Germany handled this mess, West decided to shoot low and open 1♣, which may have been a very reasonable decision. The spade fit, however, was lost in the ensuing auction.

Our 2♣ opening accomplishes no amazing feat, unless you view, as I do, unexpectedly comfortable bidding as a very worthwhile and "amazing" feat. West opens 2♣, hears 2♦ as an artificial game force, and rebids 3♣. For us, this denies a four-card major, which allows two interesting results. First, East can bid his spades (3♠) with knowledge by both partners that this promises a five-card suit, allowing Opener to raise spades without any concerns. Second, because Opener has denied a heart suit, he has an easy 4♥ alternative as his spade raise, to show general slam interest.[12]

---

[12] This specific agreement is significant for me, for an unusual reason. As a regular on the Bridge Base Online Forums, I remember a discussion about whether a natural 4♥ call by Opener in a sequence like this should be forcing, or whether Responder can pass this, as possibly the last making game. It is nice to know that discussions like this will not occur in my approach. Even if Opener has some sort of hand with something like seven clubs and four hearts, he would bid 2♠ as a relay, introduce the clubs by bidding 3♣ over 2NT, and then bid 4♣ if needed.

Would Opener opt 4♥ with this collection of values? Would Responder see the value of his diamond Ace and club King and move on? Probably not, and we would probably languish in the same 4♠ contract with two overtricks that Norway reached. However, two things are clear. First, each side is very comfortable with their bidding. Second, the only discomfort is that each smells a possible slam and just cannot muster enough to move. I like that kind of discomfort a lot more.

Minor rebids denying a four-card major can have other benefits, as well. Consider the following deal, from the 2008 World Mind Sports Games in Beijing:

```
              ♠ K Q 6 5 4
              ♥ 6 4
              ♦ K 5 3
              ♣ 7 6 4

♠ A                          ♠ 3
♥ K 10 8                     ♥ A 9 7 2
♦ A Q J 7 6                  ♦ 10 9 8 4 2
♣ A K Q J                    ♣ 10 9 2

              ♠ J 10 9 8 7 2
              ♥ Q J 5 3
              ♦ --
              ♣ 8 5 3
```

West opens 2♣, denying four spades (unless super strong). East makes a waiting 2♦ call, and, if the opponents still remain silent, West is tempted to bid 3♠ to show the minors, explained lower down on this page, but he bids 3♦. The failure to instead bid 2♠ means that

East can forget about the four-card heart suit and just support diamonds in the appropriate manner.

In practice, either North or South will eventually mess with the auction by bidding some number of spades, of course.

The Jump to Three Hearts

Opener can also jump to 3♥ as in standard methods, showing a long, self-sufficient suit and demanding cuebids. Opener will not have four spades. Of course, he might lie if his spades are lousy. There are tactical exceptions, as always in bridge.

The Jump to Three Spades

This is an interesting tool. One problem hand for standard bidders is the minor two-suiter. If you open 2♣, and then bid one of your minors (presumably diamonds) at the three-level as your next call, two bad things happen. First, Responder thinks that your suit must be a six-card suit or longer. Second, you cannot bid your other minor below 3NT. That's horrible. As a result, a 1♦ opening has a ridiculous range when Opener has both minors.

Although this is not the greatest solution in the world, it is much better. With the minor two-suiter, we can open 2♣ and then jump to 3♠ after a 2♦ response from partner. This shows 5-5 in the minors, and obviously very fewer losers.

To see this option in action, consider a problem hand from the 2007 World Championships in Shanghai. As Dealer, you hold:

♠ A ♥ A 2 ♦ A J 7 4 2 ♣ A K J 6 3

What is your plan?

Despite the 21 HCP and the great shape, most standard bidders wisely opened 1♦. Had they started with 2♣, they would have been forced to pick one of the minors to bid at the three-level for their second call, meaning that the other suit would not be bid unless they bypassed 3NT. That idea is not the solution. Rather, they opened 1♦ and hoped to catch up. The practical result was a lot of 3NT contracts after the 3♣ Jump Shift.

The full deal follows.

```
              ♠ A
              ♥ A 2
              ♦ A J 7 4 2
              ♣ A K J 6 3

♠ J 8                        ♠ K 10 7 6 5
♥ K 10 7 6 5 4               ♥ Q
♦ Q 10                       ♦ 9 6 5
♣ 9 5 4                      ♣ 10 8 7 2

              ♠ Q 9 4 3 2
              ♥ J 9 8 3
              ♦ K 8 3
              ♣ Q
```

For us, the auction to the decision point would be painless. North opens 2♣. South, whose spade suit is too poor for a positive response, bids 2♦, game forcing. North bids 3♠, in one bid describing a hand that could not otherwise be described.

Now, judgment might result in South declaring 3NT anyway, and on a different day that would be the best contract. However, on an aggressive day, we could pursue this slam, with relative comfort that we know what is going on because North has been able to place pattern and strength on the table.

How about another one? In the 2008 European Bridge Team Championships, teams faced this gem:

```
                    ♠ 5
                    ♥ A
                    ♦ A K J 10 8 3
                    ♣ K Q J 10 8

    ♠ 9 8 4 3 2                     ♠ A Q 7
    ♥ 3 2                           ♥ K Q 9 4
    ♦ 4 2                           ♦ 9 6 5
    ♣ A 9 6 3                       ♣ 7 5 2

                    ♠ K J 10 6
                    ♥ J 10 8 7 6 5
                    ♦ Q 7
                    ♣ 4
```

After a pass from West, North has one of those stupid hands that we all hate to handle. With about 2½ losers, and a lot of body in those minors, a 1♦ pass-out sequence would be infuriating, but a 2♣ opening in standard methods is ugly too.

However, consider the merits of a 2♣ opening in our methods. The predicted auction is easy. South bids 2♦, game-forcing and waiting, and North completes his basic picture in one bid – 3♠. South has a great "problem," in that he can hardly go wrong. Maybe he tries 3NT, and maybe North accepts that choice or insists on his minors. Maybe he opts the minor. Whatever he does, all roads lead to the Rome of a decent contract.

The point here is not that we would always get to the absolute best contract. The point, instead, is that the 3♠ rebid is so powerful that it makes these sequences fairly easy rather than impossibly difficult. As a result, rather than making extremely heavy 1♦ openings with minor two-suiters, like everyone else, we actually consider, for good reason, opening 2♣ with a minor two-suiter that has only 18 HCP. If we do so, the auction is easier than for standard bidders.

The Jump to 3NT

With Kokish in play, 3NT is unused. My preference is for 3NT in this sequence to be semi-gambling. I will have a long, running minor, a hand too strong to risk a one-level minor opening (because I can see nine tricks in my hand), but not much more. You can expect something like AKQ-seventh and two side Aces, and nothing more.

In the 2004 Olympiads, the Netherlands had an auction where this bid appears to have been used:

```
              ♠ K 10
              ♥ Q 8 5 4 3 2
              ♦ A K Q J
              ♣ 10

♠ A 4                        ♠ Q 7 6
♥ A 10                       ♥ K 9 7 6
♦ 5 4                        ♦ 10 6 2
♣ A K Q J 9 8 5              ♣ 7 4 2

              ♠ J 9 8 5 3 2
              ♥ J
              ♦ 9 8 7 3
              ♣ 6 3
```

West, in third seat, does not have 21 HCP, but, with nine rippers, he could not stand opening 1♣ and hearing a pass-out. I agree with that sentiment. So, he opened 2♣. After his partner bid 2♦, he jumped to 3NT, apparently showing what we would show – a running minor with two side Aces and nothing more. East might have been concerned about a minor lead, which turned out to be a valid concern, but getting to 11 tricks in five of Opener's minor seemed rightly too much to shoot for. Appropriately, East figured that 3NT was the best shot. The 4-4 diamond split helped.

That finishes the discussion of the Two Clubs opening, except, again, for handling strong, balanced hands. So, I suppose I might as well get to the discussion of the balanced hands.

A Note on 6-5 with the Majors

You may have noticed, at this point, that Opener has the ability to show a wild canapé with five spades and six of any side suit, including hearts. However, with a wild canapé that features five hearts and a six-card side suit, there is no immediate ability to show that hand except when Opener has a minor. So, you may be asking, what about hands with five hearts and six *spades*?

The problem with the 6-5 hands I have handled is that the longer suit is the higher-ranking suit. That creates rebid problems.

With six spades and five hearts, however, there is no rebid problem. You start with a 2♦ opening, expecting to rebid 2♠ if necessary, and then 3♥ if necessary, and possibly even 4♥ if necessary. These are not tough hands to bid. Thus, the "problem" is not present unless the longer suit is the lower-ranking suit.

Of course, the next question is about five diamonds and six clubs. If you have a solution for that problem, have at it. I am satisfied to at least be able to show both suits below 3NT.

SUMMARY TABLE FOR TWO CLUB OPENINGS

Opening Bid Requirements:

Shape:	Fewer than four spades unless 24+ HCP balanced
Strength:	Strong (usually 21 HCP, but occasionally light)

Responses:

2♦	artificial positive, waiting, GF
2♥	artificial negative (Opener's 2♠ then shows hearts)
2♠	positive with one or both minors; 2NT relay asks
2NT	(1) weak with minor or (2) weak with both majors
3♣	artificial positive with hearts
3♦	artificial positive with spades
3♥	weak with long hearts
3♠	weak with long spades

Opener's Rebids after 2♦ Response (artificial, GF):

2♥	Natural, 5+ hearts, unbalanced
2♠	Artificial, exactly 4 hearts, unbalanced
2NT	Natural, balanced, 22-23 HCP, only 2 or 3 spades
3♣	Long clubs (6+ unless 5♣/4♦), no 4-card major
3♦	Long diamonds (6+ unless 5♦/4♣), no 4-card major
3♥	Sets hearts as trumps, demands cuebidding
3♠	Both minors (5-5 or longer)
3NT	Running minor, tricks, but relatively weak
4♣	5♥/6+♣
4♦	5♥/6+♦

Opener's Rebids after 2♠ Rebid and 2NT Relay:

3♣	Four hearts, 5+ clubs, 0-2 spades
3♦	Four hearts, 5+ diamonds, 0-2 spades
3♥	Four hearts, 5-6 clubs, three spades
3♠	Four hearts, 5-6 diamonds, three spades
3NT	1-4-4-4
4♣	1-4-4-4 but stronger
4♦	0-4-5-4 strong
4♥	0-4-4-5 strong

WHEN OPENER SHOWS A STRONG, BALANCED HAND

The handling of strong, balanced hands within this two-way strong, forcing opening structure is astounding. Because Opener has two ways to get to 2NT with 22-23 HCP's (2♣...2NT or 2♦...2NT), each with its own inferences, Opener's delayed 2NT rebids will each have sufficiently known parameters to enable all possible major-suit exploration through Responder's 3♣ and 3♦ rebids, freeing 3♥ and 3♠ for other purposes.

You will find that no major fit can be lost. With standard methods, Stayman makes it difficult to find 5-3 fits because Responder cannot know whether Opener has four or five of the major he shows. Puppet Stayman solves that problem. However, standard Puppet Stayman presents a problem for a Responder who has five spades and four hearts. Furthermore, standard Puppet Stayman does not provide a solution when Responder has five of one major and three of the other major.

For the super-strong balanced hands, I will present a version of Puppet Stayman that solves the major-suit problem completely. For the normal strong, balanced hands, my techniques will go even further, allowing us to even explore, in one auction, the possibility of a 4-4 minor fit, below 3NT, and only after checking on the majors.

A Quick Note as to Range

When you read through these methods, you may be inclined to want to open 2♣ or 2♦ with the 20-21 HCP balanced hands, and maybe even upgraded 19-counts, because of the incredible methods available, and to open 2NT with 22-23 HCP hands. The thinking will be that 20-21 HCP hands come up way more frequently than the 22-23 HCP hands, and that you should maximize the tools for the most frequent auction. I thought of that myself.

However, this is somewhat dangerous if partner has a bust hand. When you open 2♦, and partner bids 3♥, you will be able to stop in 3♠, which might be nice. 3♠ on a 4-4 fit may be better than 2NT. When you open 2♦ and partner bids 2♥, he can pass 2NT with trash. So far, not so much risk. What about 2♣ sequences? When partner bids the bust 2♥, you will bid 2NT with these weak hands and often play there. Fine again. Same contract. Of course, now maybe partner can correct to 3♣ or 3♦, and that may be a very good thing.

However, we may be in some trouble if we get intervention. When Opener has either a shapely and strong hand, or at least 22 HCP, his playing strength is known to be high. Reducing the balanced hand to 20, or even some 19-count hands, may be too much. I remain uncertain. You decide.

When Opener Starts with Two Diamonds as His Opening

If Opener starts with a 2♦ opening, he promises at least four spades. If Opener has a balanced hand with four spades, and if Responder also has four spades, the spade fit will be found immediately, because Responder will immediately support spades. So, when Responder cannot raise spades and bids 2♥, Opener's 2NT will be bid with the understanding that a spade fit cannot exist unless Opener has five spades and with the understanding that Responder does not have a spade suit of his own. This enables a lot of options for Responder.

Quick Outline of Options after Two Diamonds Start (Opener Holds 22-23 HCP but with Four or Five Spades)

Three Clubs as Modified Puppet Stayman

Opener bids 3 ♦   = 4 ♠, 2-3 ♥, one 4+ minor

Responder can then bid *Delayed Minor-Suit Flags*
3 ♥ for 4+ clubs or both minors
3 ♠ for 4+ diamonds

Opener bids 3 ♥   = Four Hearts (and Four Spades per force)

Opener bids 3 ♠   = Five Spades

Opener bids 3NT   = 4-3-3-3 precisely

Jacoby Transfer for Hearts – Three Diamonds

Immediate Minor-Suit Flags

Three Hearts flags Clubs and shows 5+ Clubs, maybe Diamonds also

Three Spades flags Diamonds and shows 5+ Diamonds

When Responder Has a Minor and Slam Interest

As I mentioned, Responder cannot have a spade suit, so he does not need 3♥ as a transfer to spades. Many folks already use 3♠ over 3NT as a minor-oriented slam try. This is also available to Responder. Thus, Responder now has two calls for the minors.

Well, this leads to an obvious idea. If Responder bids 3♥, this is a slammish "flag" for clubs. 3♠ is a slammish flag for diamonds. Thus, Responder can show slam interest with either minor, showing the minor below 3NT. These minor-suit flags promise five-card suits.

With both minors, Responder bids 3♥ to flag clubs, which allows Opener to accept clubs by bidding something intelligent above 3NT, or to bid 3♠, with the 3♠ call at least temporarily declining clubs but suggesting interest in diamonds. Opener could also, of course, reject both minors by bidding 3NT.

Thus, Responder can bid 3♥ with just clubs or with both minors. In other words, whereas the normal 3♠ call by other folks will allow minor-suit exploration with the cost of (usually) committing us to the four-level, Responder then showing his minor or his shortness if having both minors, we will actually be able to handle much of this with calls that are below 3NT, only entering the four-level with sufficient cause.

This same thinking might also encourage you to use what would otherwise be an impossible Texas Transfer bid of 4♥ to instead allow another level of complexity, perhaps, with 4♥ showing a 3-3-3-4 quantitative and 4♠ a 3-3-4-3 quantitative, or something like that. Quantitative flags of the longer minor. Each would have the incidental benefit of allowing Opener to get out at 4♠, which might be nice if he has five spades but no interest in the slam.

Back to the three-level minor-suit flags. After a minor-suit flag, there are logical follow-up sequences that should be considered. First, consider the event of Opener declining the minor. For example, Opener hears a 3♠ flag for diamonds but bids 3NT to decline that invite. Responder can continue the slam probe naturally. He might, for instance, bid 4♣ to show continuing slam interest with both minors but longer diamonds. He might rebid diamonds to show six diamonds and continuing interest. He might even introduce a four-card heart suit, whether as a possible fit or just to complete his pattern.

Suppose, instead, that Opener accepts the minor. Opener also has options. My suggestion is to have Opener bid 4♣ to accept Responder's minor (whichever minor Responder has shown) when Opener has a suit with a hole, meaning a lack of control of some side suit. Responder can then bid a stiff major if he has one (4♥ or 4♠) or bid 4NT with a stiff in the other minor. With no stiff, Responder bids 4♦. Thus, 4♣ is initially a telling bid ("I have a fit with your minor, and slam interest, but I have a problem"), but it also is an asking bid ("Do you have a stiff?").

After this 4♣ asking/telling bid, Responder may have shown no shortness by bidding 4♦. If so, the partnership should be committed to a sort of cuebidding sequence, to ensure that this problem is resolved. If Opener cuebids 4♥, we know that the problem was in spades or in the other minor. If Responder has no control in either suit, he can sign off at game in the minor. If Responder has a control in both suits, he can bid the slam, or even probe for a possible grand if he is strong enough. If Responder has a control in spades but not in clubs, he cuebids 4♠. If Responder has a control in the other minor but not in spades, he cuebids 4NT (bypassing 4♠). Thus, a fairly straight-forward cuebidding sequence follows.

If Opener hears 4♦ and cuebids 4♠, then we know that Opener's problem suit was hearts. With no heart control, Responder signs off. With heart control, Responder bids the slam. With first-round heart control, and sufficient values, Responder might even continue a probe for a grand.

Responder might instead have shown shortness, but the wrong shortness. If so, Opener can continue to cuebid, as available, and hopefully we have space to work this out. If not, we are at least no worse than the field, who cannot possibly have resolved all of what we have resolved so far.

In the event of the wrong shortness being shown, it may be useful at times for a 4NT call to be treated as a cuebid of an unavailable suit, unless you view the natural meaning as more important. For example, if diamonds are agreed, and Responder shows a stiff spade by bidding 4♠, 5♣ by Opener would be a cuebid that isolates hearts as the hole. 4NT could then, logically, be a "cuebid" that isolates clubs as the hole.

If two suits are unavailable for cues, then 4NT, if available, could be a cue for the higher-ranking suit. Thus, imagine that clubs are agreed and that Responder shows a stiff in spades. If that was the wrong stiff, Opener could bid 4NT to cuebid hearts and infer that the hole is in diamonds, whereas a bid of 5♣, signing off, would infer that the problem was in hearts, the suit that could not be cuebid.

Back to Opener's options. If Opener has no holes, then he has two options. 4♦ agrees whichever minor Responder shows and is "Last Train," in a sense. It shows slam interest with control of every side suit and either uncertainty as to whether to bid the slam or a desire to answer rather than ask. With clear goals,

138

Opener can instead bid 4♥ as RKCB for Responder's minor. Thus, 4♥ by either side is RKCB for the agreed minor.

I suppose Opener could also bid 4♠ or something higher as some sort of picture bid. I just do not know what meaning I would remember.

One last note. Remember that if Responder bids 3♥ as a flag for clubs, Opener might reject clubs but bid 3♠ to suggest interest in a diamond slam instead, in case Responder had held both minors. After this 3♠ call, Responder can, of course, simply bid 3NT to end the auction. However, Responder has other options. He can rebid his clubs to show six of them (and reject diamonds). He can bid 4♦ to accept diamonds. Or, he can bid 4♥ or 4♠ to "super-accept" diamonds, showing five diamonds and a stiff or void in the indicated major, a splinter without the jump.

For an example of the bid in practice, consider a problem faced by Responders in the Round Robin of the World Mind Sports Games in Beijing in 2008. Partner opens 2♣ (standard) and then shows 22-23 HCP balanced after a 2♥ overcall by the opponents. You hold ♠ Q x ♥ K x ♦ 10 x x ♣ Q 7 6 5 4 2. Now, the actual situation was one where Responder lacked the club Queen, which turned out not to be an important card (clubs split 2-2). But, what can you do?

Opener actually had ♠ A K J x ♥ J x ♦ A K x x ♣ A K 10. Using our methods, Opener starts with 2♦ because he has four spades, planning to show 22-23 HCP and balanced, with four or five spades, should a spade fit not be immediately found. If the 2♥ overcall faced in Beijing still happens, any existing spade fit will be found without difficulty. In practice, however, Responder simply passes, showing a non-minimum.

When Opener rebids 2NT, now Responder has a nice call – 3♥. This serves two purposes. First, the club suit is shown. Second, Opener can assess whether he has an extra heart stopper in the event that this is needed. Note, by the way, that Responder can give full weight to his spade Queen, knowing that this supports a known suit.

In practice, Opener is very happy to reject 3NT, both because he has no heart help and because he has great club support. A reasonable continuation would be 4♣ from Opener (two of the top three clubs), 4♥ from Responder (heart control, no diamond control), 4♠ from Opener (two of the top three spades, and diamond control), 4NT by Responder (Last Train), and Opener bidding the slam.

When Responder has Interest in the Majors

Responder has two ways to ask about Opener's major holdings. He can bid the higher option of 3♦, which covers a limited variety of hands because it is more preemptive on the partnership. Or, he can bid the lower option of 3♣, which covers everything else. And, I mean just about *everything* else.

The 3♦ Jacoby Transfer

This call seems normal. Weird, eh? Responder can bid 3♦ to show five or more hearts, just like for most folks. Just like always, Opener can super-accept hearts.

However, our Jacoby Transfer auctions after a 2♦ start by Opener are admittedly special because Responder already has denied four spades by not immediately supporting Opener's known spade suit. This allows Responder to transfer to hearts by bidding

3♦ and then to bid 3♠ to show a hand with five hearts and *three* spades, checking back in case Opener has five spades with only two hearts. Thus, we solve the problem of Responder handling the 3-5 holding in the majors.

But, you can do even better, if you wish. You could make 3♠ a relay to 3NT and make 3NT show three spades, if you want to make sure that Opener declares the possible spade contract. You would then need something to show 5-3 with too good a hand to allow Opener to pass 3NT, maybe bidding 4NT instead with that hand.

In fact, if you decide to invert these meanings, then you might as well have an immediate minor call show 5-5 shape but a delayed new minor call show 5-4 shape. Thus, after a transfer to hearts, 4♣ or 4♦ would show five hearts and five of the minor, with slam interest. After a delayed 3♠ relay to 3NT, Responder could then bid a minor to show a four-card suit and slam interest. If Responder has 3514 or 3541, he could relay to 3NT and then flag his minor (4♥ for 3514 or 4♠ for 3541).

Responder also can opt to bid 4♦, instead, as a Texas Transfer to hearts, with all of the inferences you usually have in distinguishing Jacoby Transfer auctions from Texas Transfer auctions.

The Modified Puppet Stayman 3♣

Because we know that Opener, by opening 2♦, has four or five spades for his balanced hand, Puppet Stayman auctions are enhanced. I have restructured Opener's options to account for this. Because Responder has denied four spades by not immediately supporting Opener's known spade fit, this also gives Responder more options. The modified Three Clubs

141

Puppet Stayman nonetheless asks Opener about the majors.

If Opener has five spades, he bids 3♠. This is normal, and the remainder of the auction after this call is standard. I would suggest that you use 4♥ by Responder after 3♠ as Last Train, agreeing spades, however.

If Opener has four hearts, he bids 3♥. This also is fairly logical, because the presence of four known spades in Opener's hand guarantees that he will not have five hearts. You might think of this 3♣ call, then, as "Puppet Stayman for Spades but Normal Stayman for Hearts." Just to repeat, 3♥ shows four hearts and four spades. Now, there is one caveat. 4-4-4-1 and 4-4-1-4 hands are difficult for standard 2♣ openers, and our techniques do not really solve that problem ideally either. The classic solution has been to bid 2NT with these hands and hope for good things. Well, we do the same thing sometimes, when one of the alternatives discussed earlier either is not part of your arsenal or does not seem right for the hand, such as when the stiff is an honor. So, a 3♥ call occasionally might be based upon a 4-4-1-4 or 4-4-4-1 hand.

When Opener does bid 3♥, Responder can bid a minor naturally, or he can bid 3♠ as an artificial bid agreeing hearts and showing slam interest (without slam interest, he would bid 4♥, and he cannot have a spade fit). This allows Opener to bid a minor if he has a stiff (and hence disclose the 4-4-1-4 or 4-4-4-1 pattern) or to bid 3NT as a waiting call, denying a stiff minor, with normal cuebidding thereafter.

If Opener lacks five spades and lacks four hearts, he has two options. One option is a simple 3NT call, showing precisely 4-3-3-3 pattern. This call enables the call of 3♦, the other option, to guarantee a four-card minor. If Opener bids 3♦, he will have 4-2-4-3,

4-2-3-4, 4-3-4-2, or 4-3-2-4 pattern, but always a four-card minor. He might also, actually, have 4-1-4-4 pattern, if the hand seems right for this treatment or if the alternative way of handling this pattern is not available.

The 3♦ call, by promising a four-card minor, allows for an amazing follow-up. Responder now can show continuing slam interest and can look for a 4-4 minor fit, using flags. Thus, 3♥ by Responder would now flag clubs and show four or more clubs. 3♠ would flag spades and show four or more diamonds. If Opener hears 3♥ (showing four or more clubs) and has slam interest if Responder has diamonds, Opener can himself flag diamonds by bidding 3♠.

Thus, in these auctions, all four suits might be explored below 3NT. The 2♦ opening explored the possible 4-4 spade fit. Responder's eventual 3♣ call explored the possible 4-4 heart fit. After Opener's 3♦ call, Responder's 3♥ call explores a possible 4-4 club fit. After this, Opener's 3♠ call explored the last possibility of a 4-4 diamond fit.

When Opener Starts with Two Clubs as His Opening

The auctions where Opener starts with a 2♣ opening and then bids 2NT are also quite defined, because Opener now is known to have fewer than four spades. Because we can still handle all major exploration through 3♣ and 3♦, we again free up 3♥ and 3♠ for minor-suit exploration, as explained earlier. Although Responder might have a spade suit, he nonetheless does not need the Jacoby Transfer to spades, as will be seen.

So, as for the 2NT sequences after a 2♦ opening, Responder's 3♥ call is a flag for clubs or both minors, and 3♠ is a flag for diamonds.

Quick Outline of Options after Two Clubs Start (Opener Holds 22-23 HCP but with Two or Three Spades)

Three Clubs as Modified Puppet Stayman

Opener bids 3 ♦ =   2-3 ♥, 2-3 ♠, one or both 4+ minor(s)

Responder can then bid:

3 ♥ as a *Delayed Jacoby Transfer to Spades*

3 ♠ as a *Quantitative Slam Invite*

Opener bids 3 ♥   = Five Hearts

Opener bids 3 ♠   = Four Hearts and Three Spades

Opener bids 3NT   = Four Hearts and Two Spades

Jacoby Transfer for Hearts – Three Diamonds

Immediate Minor-Suit Flags

Three Hearts flags Clubs and shows 5+ Clubs, maybe Diamonds also

Three Spades flags Diamonds and shows 5+ Diamonds

The Jacoby Transfer to Hearts, and Texas Transfers

We will retain, again, the Jacoby Transfer of 3♦ to hearts. However, because Opener has denied four spades, by not opening 2♦, Responder can bid 3♠ (to show at least five spades) if Opener does not super-accept hearts. Thus, the limitation on Opener's hand means that Responder can handle 5-5 major two-suiters below 3NT.[13] If Responder gets the opportunity to complete his pattern, because of a lack of a super-acceptance of hearts by Opener, Opener can use flags (4♣ for hearts and 4♦ for spades) to show maximums, 4♥ and 4♠ instead showing preference but slam minimums.

Note, then, that a Jacoby Transfer to hearts and then bidding 3♠ shows 5♥/3♠ after a 2♦ opening but 5♥/5♠ after a 2♣ opening, all because of Opener's spade length limitations from the choice of opening bid.

As mentioned, however, we do not use a 3♥ Jacoby Transfer to spades, both because we can handle these hands through 3♣ and because we want that space for minor slam tries. This will be explained.

We also use Texas Transfers, for both majors. Sorry – no 4-3-3-3 options here.

---

[13] Again, you could invert these meanings, such that 3NT after the transfer shows 5-5 in the majors and 3♠ is a relay to 3NT, with all of the attendant benefits of distinguishing the length of an introduced second suit minor.

The Modified Puppet Stayman 3♣ after the Initial 2♣ Opening

This 3♣ call covers a lot of territory, as you will see. Opener starts by describing his hand. Remember that Opener has denied four spades.

If Opener has precisely four hearts, he shows his spade length. Thus, with four hearts, Opener bids 3♠ to show a spade fragment (four hearts and three spades) or bids 3NT to deny a spade fragment (four hearts and two spades). No matter what major pattern Responder has, he will be able to place major strains well after these calls. If Responder can rule out a major contract at this point, he can bid a minor at the four-level, natural. If Responder bids 4NT at this point, it is presumed to be in support of hearts. After 3♠ by Opener, where a spade fit is possible, Responder can jump to 5♣ as RKCB for spades. Technically, 5♣ would also be RKCB for spades after Opener's 3NT option.[14]

If Opener has five hearts, he bids 3♥. If Responder held five spades and two hearts, he could not transfer, but that is not a problem – he just bids 3♠ after Opener's 3♥ call (or, you could again invert the meanings of 3♠ and 3NT to distinguish minor lengths and to maintain the lead into Opener's hand).

If Opener has 2-3 hearts, and he is already known to have 2-3 spades, Opener bids 3♦. In this sequence, however, Responder cannot now use flag bids to seek out possible minor fits. That is because we have abandoned the 3♥ Jacoby Transfer. Instead, Responder can, if Responder has five or more spades, *now* transfer to spades by bidding 3♥. If Responder bids 3♥ as a transfer to spades, Opener can super-accept with three-

---

[14] One could also use transfers here, with 4♠ showing clubs.

card support. This may seem contorted, bidding 3♣ first and then transferring later, but it is a level of complexity that does gain the ability to explore the minors with a consistent treatment.

After this 3♦ bid by Opener, Responder can also make a general slam move of 3♠, which encourages Opener to bid a minor if he has a maximum. If Opener dislikes his hand for slam, he can suggest a sign-off by bidding 3NT. Thus, 3♠ is a general punt that shows at least mild slam interest and encourages Opener to join the discussion.

Consider these hands from the 2008 World Mind Sports Games:

Opener: ♠ A Q 4 ♥ A 3 2 ♦ A K 10 5 2 ♣ A J
Responder: ♠ K J 10 2 ♥ J 7 ♦ Q 9 8 ♣ Q 7 3 2

Opener starts with 2♣, like everyone else, but our Responder already knows that no spade fit exists. After a 2♦ waiting bid seen all around the room, our Opener, like others, rebids 2NT.

Here, however, differences emerge. Everyone playing a standard 2♣ will now have a Puppet Stayman sequence where Responder will bid 3♣ and hear a 3NT rebid, denying a four-card major. Then, a decision.

Our Responder has two options. One option is that he could just bid 4NT quantitative, if he thinks the hand strong enough, without the need for the Puppet Stayman sequence. Alternatively, Responder could bid 3♣ as Modified Puppet Stayman. If Opener bids 3♦, this allows Responder to bid 3♠ as quantitative, which saves a level of bidding, and that is always a good thing for slam exploration. If Opener instead bids anything else, Responder could now bid 4NT and will have just delayed things, or he could back down and just sign off at 3NT.

In practice, if Responder opts to bid 3♣, he will be rewarded with that 3♦ call and can make his slam move without committing to going past 3NT. Whether Opener accepts or not, and whether this slam makes or not, is immaterial to Responder's relief of being able to avoid the do-I-or-don't-I wiggle and dance.

Deals from Actual Play

Consider a deal that caused problems in 2007 at the World Championships:

```
              ♠ K J 6
              ♥ A K 10 7 6
              ♦ A K
              ♣ A 10 3

♠ --                        ♠ Q 10 9 7 5 3
♥ 9 4 3 2                   ♥ Q J 5
♦ J 9 7 6 5 4              ♦ 10
♣ Q 9 6                     ♣ J 5 2

              ♠ A 8 4 2
              ♥ 8
              ♦ Q 8 3 2
              ♣ K 8 7 4
```

West deals and passes. North has a very strong 22 HCP, balanced hand. I might almost consider this worth as much as 24 HCP's because of the great five-card suit and the primes, but it is clearly worth at least 23. Either way, though, we would open 2♣, either because this is a super-strong balanced hand (24+) or

148

because it is a normal 22-23 HCP balanced hand with fewer than four spades.

South has a clear game-forcing response without any available positive, so he bids 2♦. Now, had North upgraded this hand wildly, to the super-strong balanced range, he could bid 2♥, intended as a Kokish relay to 2♠. Responder could reject that suggestion and bid 3♥, showing a 4-1-4-4 hand. That would have been nice, but our Opener makes the sane 2NT bid. He is allowed to have a maximum.

What does Responder do now? Well, there cannot be a heart fit. Further, because Opener did not open 2♦, he has denied four spades, so no spade fit is possible. If Opener happens to have a four-card minor, a minor slam does seem possible. We would have 31-32 HCP's, with a distributional value.

Responder would have two options that make some sense. He could simply opt to leave the opponents in the dark and bid 3NT. Or, Responder might also bid 3♣ to ask about Opener's majors. A 3♥ response (five hearts) would convince him to sign off. A 3♠ response (3♠/4♥) would be somewhat discouraging but a 3NT response (2♠/4♥) would be somewhat encouraging, leaving Responder more intelligent in his guessing as to whether to move on or sign off. A 3♦ response would be great, as it would allow Responder to bid an artificial 3♠ to show at least mild slam interest and to encourage Opener to bid a minor.

If I were Responder, the choice would be simple. I would bid 3♣ and hope for the 3♦ response, so I could explore the minors, or a 3♥ response, which would shut this thing down immediately. I would get my lesser wish of the 3♥ call and would end the auction at 3NT.

A damned shame, though. We sure would have been the talk of Shanghai had we found a 4-4 minor fit in diamonds if Opener had a 3-3-4-3 pattern with the exact same honors. He would have bid 3♦ in response to my 3♣ asking bid; I would have bid 3♠ as a general invite; and then he would have established the diamond fit. That would have given me confidence to pursue and ultimately bid the slam. I would need diamonds to be 3-2, with either the spade Queen on side or spades 3-3, or the club Queen-Jack being tight, or a spade-club squeeze, a typical slam for me, but wow if it came home! The IBPA would go nuts!

Another set of hands from Shanghai would result in a normal contract but is worthwhile to study as an example of how we would bid.

Opener: ♠ A K Q ♥ A J ♦ Q J 10 5 4 ♣ A J 9
Responder: ♠ 10 8 4 3 2 ♥ 10 ♦ 9 8 7 6 ♣ K Q 6

Opener, with 22 HCP's and balanced, opens 2♣ on route to 2NT, 2♣ because he does not have four spades. Responder has enough to force game, but not a positive with a suit, so he bids 2♦. Opener bids 2NT, showing 22-23 HCP.

Responder cannot transfer to spades, because 3♥ shows a slammish hand and a club suit (a flag for clubs). So, he goes through 3♣, asking about Opener's major holdings. If Opener were to bid 3♠ to show 4♥/3♠, Responder would bid 4♠ (or 4♥ as a transfer to 4♠ if you like that idea). If Opener were to bid 3NT to show 4♥/2♠, Responder would pass. If Opener were to bid 3♥ to show five hearts, Responder would bid 3♠ to show five spades (or 3NT if you like the inversions).

However, Opener has fewer than four hearts, and he has already shown fewer than four spades, so Opener bids 3♦. Responder now can transfer to spades by bidding 3♥ and then bid 3NT as a choice of games. Opener will correct to 4♠, declining to cuebid anything on the way because his overall hand is not that good for slam purposes.

A simple hand from Pau is also worth considering. As Responder, you are dealt ♠ J 8 4 2 ♥ A 2 ♦ 10 9 7 2 ♣ K 8 3. Partner opens 2♣, you respond 2♦, and partner rebids 2NT. For most, Stayman or Puppet Stayman comes to mind. However, you know that Opener does not have four spades, because he opened 2♣ and not 2♦. Sure, maybe there is a diamond slam (there was), but who finds that (no one did)? Make the practical call of 3NT immediately rather than the wildly aggressive 3♠ diamond flag, which would show five diamonds anyway. Sure, maybe you could bid 3♣, hoping for a 3♦ rebid (not four hearts), and *then* bid 3♠ to show slam interest with at least *four* diamonds, but that diamond suit is lousy.

The improved handling of the majors would have landed us in a very interesting contract in the 2007 European Open Pairs Championship:

```
                ♠ Q 7 5
                ♥ Q J 9 6
                ♦ Q 6 4 3
                ♣ 9 2

  ♠ A 9                          ♠ J 10 8 6 4
  ♥ A K 10 3 2                   ♥ 9 8 5
  ♦ A 10 5                       ♦ K 8
  ♣ A Q 7                        ♣ 10 8 4

                ♠ K 3 2
                ♥ 4
                ♦ J 9 7 2
                ♣ K J 6 5 3
```

After two passes, West opens 2♣ because his 21 HCP, with two 10's and a good 5-card suit, is clearly worthy of an upgrade.   East, with a King, bids 2♦, waiting and game forcing. Opener rebids 2NT.

At this point, most people would transfer to spades and then bid 3NT, losing the heart suit. We, however, would bid 3♣ to ask about Opener's majors, as Opener has denied four spades and as we can easily find a 3-5 spade fit through 3♣.   On this hand, however, Opener rebids 3♥ to show the five-card heart suit, and we find that fit that many others miss.

The play is also interesting. Suppose that North leads a passive club, for instance. After winning the club Ace or Queen as needed, West could cross to the diamond King to take a heart finesse. When that loses and a black card is returned, the diamond Ace and a diamond ruff allows another heart despite the nice sequence.

Alternatively, though, Opener might smell a rat for some reason. When he wins the club, he could then duck a spade to whomever. Suppose any card but a trump from South comes back. West can then cash the remaining high black honor(s) in his hand, plus two top trumps, finding the bad news. He can then cross to dummy with the diamond King and ruff a spade. Diamond Ace and a third diamond is ruffed on dummy to lead the established spade for a club pitch, ruffed by North with the heart Jack. Making four.

Which line is better is for the play technicians. I am just happy that I have the chance to make this play rather than languishing in what looks like a hopeless 3NT.

A deal from the 2007 United States Bridge Championship illustrates both the value of the pattern limitations and the use of flags for the minors.

♠ J 10 4 3
♥ J 8 6
♦ 8 2
♣ 10 7 5 2

♠ A Q 8 6	♠ K 9
♥ 10 5	♥ A K 7 4
♦ J 7 6 5 3	♦ A K 4
♣ A 3	♣ K J 6 4

♠ 7 5 2
♥ Q 9 3 2
♦ Q 10 9
♣ Q 9 8

East deals and opens 2♣, planning to rebid 2NT. Sure, he only has 21 HCP, but with eight controls, an upgrade of 1 HCP is not unreasonable, as he is not flat and his cards are all working. I would open 2♣ in a heartbeat, as I have the extra advantage, as well, of the enhanced structure that we play if I can show 22 HCP. Plus, I open a lot of 19-count 2NT bids.

Responder bids 2♦ because he has a positive response but no biddable suit. Opener rebids 2NT, showing this hand and denying four spades.

Back to Responder. Opener has already ruled out a spade fit, and Responder knows that a heart fit is out as well. With 11 HCP, though, slam should be close. It seems appropriate to introduce the diamonds. Responder therefore uses the flag bid of 3♠ to show slam interest with five diamonds.

Opener obviously has interest when he is looking at the Ace and King of trumps. So, he can show diamond support with interest. The remaining route to slam is easy to see. Opener can bid 4♦ to agree diamonds and show that he has control of all side suits, if he considers that this situation calls for caution. This works out nicely, as Responder will know after Opener's answer to a 4♥ RKCB bid by West that Opener has the Ace and King of diamonds, the heart Ace, and both black Kings. Alternatively, Opener could himself bid 4♥ as RKCB.

Imagine if the spade Queen and King were swapped and the club Ace and King also. In that case, Opener with ♠ Q 9 ♥ A K 7 4 ♦ A K 4 ♣ A J 6 4; Responder with ♠ A K 8 6 ♥ 10 5 ♦ J 7 6 5 3 ♣ K 3. With that hand, Opener would have bid 4♣ instead of 4♦, accepting clubs but advertising a control hole to fill, asking for a shortness bid. Because Responder does not have a singleton, which he would have bid (or 4NT with a stiff club), he bids 4♦. Opener then starts cuebidding, starting with 4♥ to show the heart control and to isolate that the problem is in one of the black suits. Responder, holding control in both black suits, can then simply bid 6♦, as a grand seems very remote.

Another example from the 2008 United States Bridge Championships, from the Nickell-Welland match:

```
              ♠ 8 7 5
              ♥ J 9 5 3 2
              ♦ 8
              ♣ K J 8 4

♠ A K 10                      ♠ Q 9 2
♥ A 8 7                       ♥ Q 10 4
♦ A 10                        ♦ K Q J 7 2
♣ A Q 9 6 3                   ♣ 10 7

              ♠ J 6 4 3
              ♥ K 6
              ♦ 9 6 5 4 3
              ♣ 5 2
```

West deals and opens 2♣ because he has a full 21 HCP, with prime values and a good five-card trick source. East could, at this point, make a positive response in diamonds by bidding an immediate 2♠, as you recall, but he really should have a sixth diamond for that action. Instead, he takes the passive route of 2♦, waiting and game forcing. Opener rebids 2NT.

At this point, we have had the same sequence that most would have, although some may have skipped the 2♣ and the 2♦ calls if they do not upgrade as much as I do. But, we now have a serious advantage, in that East already knows that there is no spade fit. That reduces by half the merits of Puppet Stayman as his first action, which many may use here, planning to bid 4♦ later.

East has two options, nonetheless. The option in the USBC at two tables was to bid 3♠, presumably as a slam move with one or both minors. Some tweak this in a nice way by allowing Opener to show general disinterest (3NT) or general interest (4♣), Even that idea suffers from a lack of knowledge by Opener as to what he may or may not be interested in, Responder has done little to explain his hand other than to focus on one or both minors. To complete his picture, East must make another call, bypassing 3NT.

However, East actually has two good options, as I said, if using our techniques. First, he could use our version of Puppet Stayman to check on a possible 5-card heart suit. If Opener does show five hearts (3♥), that fit is found and the focus can change to exploring a heart slam, with Responder having a nice non-trump trick source. If Opener shows exactly four hearts (whether 3♠ for four hearts and three spades or 3NT for four hearts and two spades), Responder is in the same situation as others who might use normal Puppet Stayman, in that he must bid 4♦ if he wants to continue the slam probe. However, if Opener has only two or three hearts, Opener will bid 3♦, which allows a delayed diamond flag of 3♠ to show at least four diamonds and slam interest. If Opener has four diamonds and slam interest, a nine-card fit will be found, a good thing. If Opener declines the diamond slam try, Responder could make one more stab at the slam by repeating his diamonds, back with everyone else.

Alternatively, Responder could take the same practical course as adopted by the Nickell and Welland teams, namely focusing the diamonds without checking back on any possible major fits. Our auction, however, will be a slightly better auction. Responder will, in that plan, bid an immediate 3♠ over Opener's 2NT rebid to show slam interest with five diamonds. Not only will we gain by having Opener makes his decision as to interest or non-interest by looking at his diamond support and knowing what the focus will be, which must help, but Opener can even kick into our special bids of 4♣ and 4♦, as the diamond suit is known to be the focus minor. Move one of Opener's heart pips to diamonds and Opener would cooperate with a 4♦ call (showing control in all side suits), or maybe even an immediate 4♥ (RKCB for diamonds). Of course, the end would be disappointing, but sometimes slams fail.

Note that our two-way flag structure suffers no deficiency to the method of a 3♠ relay when Responder has both minors and, in the usual methods, can then bid his major to isolate the stiff. We do much better even with those hands.

First of all, in the situation of Opener starting with a 2♣ opening and a 2NT rebid, Responder will already have had a chance to make a two-minor positive with a *Two Spades* relay, (and a bid of his stiff *at the three-level*), saving an entire level of bidding.

Second, in the situation of Opener starting with a 2♦ opening and a 2NT rebid, Responder bids 3♥ to flag clubs with the 5-5 minor hands. If Opener likes and agrees clubs, he will be able to immediately focus our trump fit and either ask for the stiff (bidding 4♣), if he cares, or show club support with all suits controlled if he does not (bidding 4♦, or 4♥ as RKCB for clubs). If Opener declines clubs, he can instead propose diamonds by flagging diamond acceptance values (3♠), after which Responder will agree with this suggestion by *now* bidding his stiff minor. In that auction, Responder makes the same 4♥ or 4♠ call as in the traditional methods, but both sides now know that the trump suit is already agreed as being diamonds, knowledge that no one else has. That establishment of strain allows the next-up bid to be RKCB for diamonds and allows Last

Train and other slam probe bids below game in diamonds.

Third, after the 2♣ auction, Responder might even be able to make a slam try with both minors and not quite enough for an immediate positive, in the same enhanced manner as with 2♦ openings.

Finally, note that we also can make four-card minor slam tries below 3NT, delayed 5-4 and 4-5 minor slam tries, two-call auctions in one minor (flag-3NT-repeat minor), and the like, sequences that are not available for other bidders.

When Opener Has the Super Balanced Hand and Bids 2NT after Kokish

In this sequence, we no longer have any of the enhancements of knowing something already about Opener's spade holding. In this event, you can use whatever your normal approach is. I do have a preference, however.

My style uses Jacoby Transfers and Texas Transfers.

Quick Outline of Options for 24+ Balanced

Three Clubs as Modified Puppet Stayman
>   Opener bids 3♦ =   2-3♥, 2-4♠
>   Responder can then bid:
>   3♥ asks for Spade length
>   3♠ asks for Heart length
>   Opener bids 3♥   = Four or Five Hearts
>   (3♠ asks)
>   Opener bids 3♠   = Five Spades
>   Opener bids 3NT   = Four Hearts and Four
>   Spades
Jacoby Transfer for Hearts – Three Diamonds
Jacoby Transfer for Spades – Three Hearts
Minor-Suit Slam Try – Three Spades
>   Opener bids 3NT with little interest
>   Opener bids 4♣ with slam interest
>   Responder bids
>   Step One   = Clubs
>   Step Two   = Diamonds
>   Step Three   = Both Minors, Short Hearts
>   Step Four   = Both Minors, Short Spades
>   Next Step   = 2245/2254, maybe defining
>   long minor

Three Spades as a Minor-Oriented Asking Bid

My 3♠ call is an asking bid. If Opener has a hand that generally looks good for some or all minor-oriented slam tries, he bids 4♣. If Opener is hesitant, he bids 3NT. If Opener bids 3NT, Responder can bid a minor (4♣ or 4♦) with a one-suited minor slam try, or Responder can bid his short major with both minors and slammish, or Responder might bid 4NT with 2-2-4-5/2-2-5-4 and quantitative. If Opener bids 4♣, Responder bumps his bids up one degree (4♦ is a one-suited club slam try; 4♥ is a one-suited diamond slam try; 4♠ is a two-suited minor slam try with a stiff heart; 4NT is a two-suited slam try with a stiff spade, and Responder bids his longer minor at the five-level with 2-2-4-5 or 2-2-5-4 and quantitative). Responder also might simply pass if Opener bids 3NT or bid 6NT if Opener bids 4♣.

Modified Puppet Stayman

I also use a modified version of Puppet Stayman in this sequence. 3♣ asks about the majors. If Opener has both four-card majors, he bids 3NT. If Opener has five spades, he bids 3♠. If Opener has four or five hearts, but not four spades, he bids 3♥; in that event, Responder can ask if Opener has five hearts by bidding 3♠. If Opener has 2-3 hearts and 2-4 spades, he bids 3♦. If Responder hears 3♦ and wants to know how many hearts Opener has, Responder bids 3♠, with Opener's 3NT showing two and other bids showing three. If Responder hears 3♦ and wants to know how many spades Opener has, Responder bids 3♥; Opener bids 3NT with two spades, 3♠ with three spades, or higher bids with four spades.

This Modified Puppet Stayman allows us to find all major fits and makes Opener declare all contracts.

However, this Puppet Stayman has two problem hands for Responder.

If Responder has five hearts and four spades, his modified Puppet Stayman does not work, because Responder cannot handle the 3♦ response. With that hand, though, Responder would use a simple Jacoby Transfer to hearts and then bid 3♠ (or 3NT is you are obsessed about these inversions).

The other problem hand is when Responder has five spades and three hearts, because Responder will not be able to field the 3♥ response from Opener if spades is actually the fit. The solution is again a Jacoby Transfer, this time to spades. However, Opener is authorized to decline the transfer and to bid 3NT instead when Opener has two spades and five hearts – problem solved.

The other benefit to Puppet Stayman is that a lot of auctions allow Opener to super-accept and to cuebid in support of the to-be-agreed major. I like it enough to use it after 2NT openings, but that is a tad more dangerous because it deprives us of the ability to sign off at 3♠ when Responder has a weak hand with long spades. I consider that cost worth the gains.

A few from actual play

It was fairly normal to reach 6NT on these hands in Shanghai:

Opener: ♠ A J ♥ A K Q 4 ♦ A K 9 8 ♣ Q J 7
Responder: ♠ K Q 8 3 ♥ 7 6 2 ♦ Q J 7 ♣ K 10 5

The matching minor Q-J-7's must have been the key. Our bidding would reach the same result, but the bidding is worth reviewing nonetheless. Opener opens 2♣ because he has a super-strong balanced hand. Responder has a game-forcing hand without a suit, so he bids 2♦. Opener starts the Kokish Relay with 2♥. Responder, who does not have any 4-4-4-1 pattern, obliges with the expected relay and bids 2♠. Opener completes his picture by bidding 2NT. In this one auction, Opener might now have as many as four or five spades.

Responder is interested in whether Opener does have four or five spades and is interested in whether Opener has five hearts. So, he bids 3♣ to ask about Opener's majors. Opener responds 3♥ to show four or five hearts with fewer than four spades. Well, spades are out. So, Responder checks back on Opener's heart length by bidding 3♠. Opener bids 3NT because he only has four hearts.

That auction might seem like a lot for something so simple. But, what if Responder had held *five* spades and Opener had held *five* hearts?

Opener: ♠ A J ♥ A K Q 4 3 ♦ A K 9 ♣ Q J 7
Responder: ♠ K Q 8 3 2 ♥ 7 6 2 ♦ Q J 7 ♣ K 10

Then, Responder would have bid 3♥ as a transfer to spades instead of 3♣, but Opener would have rejected the transfer and bid 3NT instead to show five hearts and only two spades. That would have allowed us to discover the heart fit.

What if Opener had held two hearts and five spades, and Responder three spades and five hearts?

Opener: ♠ A K Q 4 3 ♥ A J ♦ A K 9 ♣ Q J 7
Responder: ♠ 7 6 2 ♥ K Q 8 3 2 ♦ Q J 7 ♣ K 10

This is more interesting. Now, Responder will not transfer. Instead, Responder bids 3♣. If Opener were to bid 3♥, the enormous heart fit is found. After

3NT, both majors, the heart fit is found. So far, no problems.

If Opener bids 3♦, showing 2-4 spades and 2-3 hearts, there is no problem because a spade fit is no longer possible. So, Responder just would ask for clarification of the heart length (by bidding 3♠). Opener will move past 3NT when he holds three hearts. Again, no problem.

In practice, Opener bids 3♠. Responder does not know if Opener has two hearts or three hearts, but the spade fit is found, and that works fine.

Another deal from Shanghai:

```
              ♠ Q 9 2
              ♥ 9 7 6 2
              ♦ Q 8 6 2
              ♣ 9 4

♠ 6 4 3                      ♠ 7 5
♥ 10 4                       ♥ Q 8 5 3
♦ J 9 7 3                    ♦ 10 5 4
♣ A 7 6 2                    ♣ K J 8 3

              ♠ A K J 10 8
              ♥ A K J
              ♦ A K
              ♣ Q 10 5
```

South opens 2♣. Sure, he has four or more spades, but this is the super-strong balanced hand that calls for the Kokish Relay and an exception to the general rule that 2♣ denies four or more spades.

Responder, with two Queens, has just barely enough for a 2♦ response. That allows Opener to bid

2♥ as a Kokish Relay. Responder, who does not have 4-4-4-1 pattern, complies by bidding 2♠. Opener completes his pattern description and shows the super-strong balanced hand by now bidding 2NT.

Responder bids 3♣ to check on majors, and Opener shows his five spades by bidding 3♠. Responder bid 4♠ to show the dead minimum; with slam interest, Responder could have bid 4♥, instead. Note that Responder would have bid this the same way if he had held a fifth heart, which would have been critical had Opener held only two hearts.

HANDLING INTERFERENCE

I am sure that at some point you must have wondered whether all of this can withstand interference. Actually, this is yet another benefit of this approach. You have already seen a few hands where this is shown to be the case. As a simple example, consider three possible methods and one identical intervening bid.

At Table 1, North, holding a 22 HCP hand with 4-3-6-0 shape, opens 1♣. East intervenes with a 4♣ overcall. South, with 4-3-2-4 shape and the King of spades as his only card, has a fairly clear pass. Getting to 4♠ now would be quite impressive.

At Table 2, North is playing 2/1 GF and opens 2♣ with this same hand. A 4♣ overcall again greets South. There is some advantage here, in that South knows that game is probably on. But, finding that spade fit is still a daunting task. A few will land on their feet after a pass from South and a reopening double by North. If West kicks this up to 5♣ first, North will hardly opt 5♠ over 5♦.

At Table 3, North is using our methods and opens 2♦. After a 5♣ overcall by East, one level higher, South has cause to actually consider 5♠. If he declines, Opener's 5♦ can be converted. Notice how nice it is for Opener to be able to show at least nine of his cards in this sequence, by the way. A 4♣ overcall, what everyone else received, is laughed off as trivial.

I am sure that you see my point. That said, the matter still calls for some discussion and agreements.

Interference After a Two Diamond Opening

When we open 2♦ and hear interference, we are obviously in a superior position over the field because Opener has already placed four spades on the table.

This may result in Responder being enabled to automatically establish spades as trumps. But, beyond that, this also allows Opener a lot more freedom to complete the picture of his hand, as it is a lot easier to describe difficult two-suited hands in competition when one of the suits is already known.

Responder's Options After 2♦ if Doubled

If the opponents double 2♦, Responder uses essentially the same style, for the most part. However, a few little space-saving ideas make sense.

First, instead of just bidding 2♥ as the relay, Responder has two options, namely passing or redoubling. The approach can be for the most part standard, with a redouble showing a bust hand and a pass showing a positive, but both without spade support.

I would also recommend that 2♥ be used to show a heart positive instead of 2♠. In that event, a good meaning for 2♠ might be positive but with 0 or 1 spades. That would make a pass promise two or three spades.

Everything else should remain the same, including the jumps in support of spades, with three possible exceptions.

This double might be takeout of spades, in which case nothing is different. I doubt that the double will be played as "Majors" and come up, but if it does then I would suggest ignoring this claim that it shows spades as possibly fictitious and treat this as showing hearts. It might show a suit. If it shows a suit, or a two-suited hand with an anchor suit, then I would suggest that a cuebid, if that call would usually be a positive bid in a suit, instead show a positive raise of spades with shortness in the opponents' suit.

Also, if the double shows a specific minor, then 3♠ by Responder, usually showing the minors, should instead show a "fit jump" in the other minor. For example, if the double shows diamonds, then Responder could bid 3♠ with 5-7 HCP's with clubs and a spade fit.

The third possible exception is that you may want to use immediate jumps into suits that the intervener has not shown as fit bids (real suits plus support) rather than as shortness bids. That may be more in line with those of us who like the methods advocated by Andrew Robson and Oliver Segal in their brilliant work, *Partnership Bidding at Bridge*. These fit bids should probably be based on limited hands, as well.

Responder's Options After a 2♥ Overcall

This call also does little to preempt us. I would suggest the same split between double and redouble as after the pass. If 2♥ shows the obvious – hearts – then 2♠ could again show a positive with a stiff or void in spades, limiting the pass to a hand with two or three spades. Note that 3♥ in this sequence would not be a shortness positive, as that call is needed to show the simple minimal raise of spades.

Also, I would suggest that the 3♠ response, usually showing both minors and limited values, be used instead to show the positive splinter, meaning a positive with shortness in hearts, rather than the usual meaning.

If 2♥ shows some other suit, and not hearts, then 3♠ should be a positive splinter with shortness in the suit intervener actually possesses, and then 2♠ should probably revert to its normal meaning as a heart positive.

Responder's Options After a 2♠ Overcall

This undoubtedly is a Michaels type of call. If it is, then pass and double should retain the same meanings as described above. 3♠ should be the positive splinter, and in hearts. If the second suit is known, then a bid of that suit should also be a positive splinter, but short in that other suit.

Responder's Options After a 2NT Overcall

This will undoubtedly show the minors. Unusual versus unusual makes some sense, to a limited degree. I would still have 3♥ as a minimal spade raise, reserving 3♦ for stronger spade raises. 3♣ would flag hearts in this method. 3♠ would be a positive splinter with shortness in one of the minors, with 3NT asking if Opener has the space.

Responder's Options After Higher Interference

If the opponents make higher calls, Responder should make more natural calls. Thus, after 3♣, I would expect 3♦ and 3♥ to both be natural, with 3♠ showing just spades and not enough to bid game. 4♣, the cue, would be a power raise of spades, and jumps would be either splinters or fit jumps according to your preferred style. It is at about this level, the 3♣ call, where you really may need to be more natural in your approach and forget about protecting the lead.

There are some possible ideas for the daring, however. I am describing these separately.

Special Idea after 3♣ or 3♦ Interference –
Submarine Style

You could still use a transferring approach, where Responder now switches into submarine style. This would be a little complicated, but I will try to explain.

Consider, for example, the 3♣ overcall. Using submarine style, Responder bids one below his natural option, wrapping around at the point right before the cuebid:

3♦	= shows hearts
3♥	= raises spades
3♠	= transfers to 3NT
3NT	= shows clubs
4♣	= power spade raise
4♦	= jump showing fit, whether shortness or fit-jump

Similarly, consider a submarine approach after 3♦:

3♥	= raises spades
3♠	= transfers to 3NT
3NT	= shows clubs
4♣	= shows hearts
4♦	= power raise of spades
4♥	= jump showing fit, whether shortness or fit-jump

After 3♥ or Higher

After competition this high, you probably need to go natural, with a cuebid, if available, as a power raise. After 3NT for the minors, Unusual Versus Unusual makes sense, however. You may also want to consider whether it might be worthwhile to have a double, especially after 3♥ specifically, be used as a "Support Double," promising three spades, typically with ability to field a completion by Opener of his canapé when he has four spades and a longer second suit.

Opener's Options

When Opener rebids, you should have some general expectations as to what he should do. As a general rule, however, Opener tends to rebid in his second suit when he has a longer second suit and tends to double or rebid spades when he has longer spades, although at times Opener just has to bid his second suit whether it be equal, longer, or shorter.

After a double of 2♦, passed or redoubled back to Opener, then, Opener would tend to bid 2♥ when he has longer hearts than spades. The rest of the approach is as if there was no interference. In the case of a heart overcall, we are in the same sequence as if Responder has bid 2♥, except that Responder has also been able to define something about his strength. So, Opener's approach is normal.

However, suppose that a higher preempt is passed back to partner, like a 3♣ overcall. If Opener bids 3♦ or 3♥, these would tend to show his longer suit. With five spades and four diamonds or four hearts, Opener would tend to reopen with a double, planning to convert the contract if Responder picks wrong. How about a 3♦ overcall? Opener would tend to reopen with 3♥ if hearts is his longer suit but to double with five spades and four or five hearts. With spades and clubs, Opener would typically rebid 4♣ with longer clubs but rebid 3♠ with five spades and four clubs. When Opener has five spades and five of a second suit, tactics may cause Opener to bid these hands either as if he has longer spades or longer in the second suit.

Interference After a Two Clubs Opening

When we open 2♣ and hear interference, we are still better off than the field, because Opener *usually* does not have four or more spades. For the most part, however, we are relatively stuck with normal methods, because Opener does not in any way promise a heart suit and because his options are still wildly varied.

However, if Opener does get the chance to reopen at a level that is low enough for all of his ideal structure to be employed, all of the structure is employed. Thus, after 2♣-2♦-P-P, Opener can still bid 2♠, for instance, to show a four-card heart suit and unbalanced, whether with a longer minor or with 1-4-4-4 shape.

CPSIA information can be obtained at www.ICGtesting.com
Printed in the USA
LVOW031318021111

253206LV00002B/2/P